The Habsburg Empire: A Very Short Introduction

VERY SHORT INTRODUCTIONS are for anyone wanting a stimulating and accessible way into a new subject. They are written by experts, and have been translated into more than 45 different languages.

The series began in 1995, and now covers a wide variety of topics in every discipline. The VSI library now contains over 500 volumes—a Very Short Introduction to everything from Psychology and Philosophy of Science to American History and Relativity—and continues to grow in every subject area.

Very Short Introductions available now:

ACCOUNTING Christopher Nobes
ADOLESCENCE Peter K. Smith
ADVERTISING Winston Fletcher
AFRICAN AMERICAN RELIGION
   Eddie S. Glaude Jr
AFRICAN HISTORY John Parker and
   Richard Rathbone
AFRICAN RELIGIONS
   Jacob K. Olupona
AGEING Nancy A. Pachana
AGNOSTICISM Robin Le Poidevin
AGRICULTURE Paul Brassley and
   Richard Soffe
ALEXANDER THE GREAT
   Hugh Bowden
ALGEBRA Peter M. Higgins
AMERICAN HISTORY Paul S. Boyer
AMERICAN IMMIGRATION
   David A. Gerber
AMERICAN LEGAL HISTORY
   G. Edward White
AMERICAN POLITICAL HISTORY
   Donald Critchlow
AMERICAN POLITICAL PARTIES
   AND ELECTIONS L. Sandy Maisel
AMERICAN POLITICS Richard M. Valelly
THE AMERICAN PRESIDENCY
   Charles O. Jones
THE AMERICAN REVOLUTION
   Robert J. Allison
AMERICAN SLAVERY
   Heather Andrea Williams
THE AMERICAN WEST Stephen Aron
AMERICAN WOMEN'S HISTORY
   Susan Ware

ANAESTHESIA Aidan O'Donnell
ANARCHISM Colin Ward
ANCIENT ASSYRIA Karen Radner
ANCIENT EGYPT Ian Shaw
ANCIENT EGYPTIAN ART AND
   ARCHITECTURE Christina Riggs
ANCIENT GREECE Paul Cartledge
THE ANCIENT NEAR EAST
   Amanda H. Podany
ANCIENT PHILOSOPHY Julia Annas
ANCIENT WARFARE Harry Sidebottom
ANGELS David Albert Jones
ANGLICANISM Mark Chapman
THE ANGLO-SAXON AGE John Blair
ANIMAL BEHAVIOUR
   Tristram D. Wyatt
THE ANIMAL KINGDOM
   Peter Holland
ANIMAL RIGHTS David DeGrazia
THE ANTARCTIC Klaus Dodds
ANTISEMITISM Steven Beller
ANXIETY Daniel Freeman and
   Jason Freeman
THE APOCRYPHAL GOSPELS
   Paul Foster
ARCHAEOLOGY Paul Bahn
ARCHITECTURE Andrew Ballantyne
ARISTOCRACY William Doyle
ARISTOTLE Jonathan Barnes
ART HISTORY Dana Arnold
ART THEORY Cynthia Freeland
ASIAN AMERICAN HISTORY
   Madeline Y. Hsu
ASTROBIOLOGY David C. Catling
ASTROPHYSICS James Binney

For more information visit our website

www.oup.com/vsi/

Martyn Rady

THE HABSBURG EMPIRE

A Very Short Introduction

OXFORD
UNIVERSITY PRESS

OXFORD
UNIVERSITY PRESS

Great Clarendon Street, Oxford, OX2 6DP,
United Kingdom

Oxford University Press is a department of the University of Oxford.
It furthers the University's objective of excellence in research, scholarship,
and education by publishing worldwide. Oxford is a registered trade mark of
Oxford University Press in the UK and in certain other countries

Published in the United States of America by Oxford University Press
198 Madison Avenue, New York, NY 10016, United States of America

British Library Cataloguing in Publication Data
Data available

Library of Congress Control Number: 2016954117

ISBN 978-0-19-879296-3

Printed in Great Britain by
Ashford Colour Press Ltd., Gosport, Hampshire.

Contents

Acknowledgements

Simon Dixon, Rebecca Haynes, and Alan Sked read the complete
text and I am most grateful for their suggestions and corrections.
I also owe much to the anonymous readers of OUP and to OUP's
Terka Acton and Jenny Nugée. Christopher Brennan, Egbert
Klautke, and Anastazja Grudnicka read portions of earlier drafts and
made valuable comments. Natalia Nowakowska was kind enough
to invite me to the conference on Dynasty and Dynasticism, held
in March 2016 in Oxford, as part of the international Jagiellonians
project, which helped me refine some of my thinking.

My principal debt is to Trevor Thomas. We have for a quarter of a
century spent many evenings together discussing the Habsburg
Empire, and I have borrowed freely from his storehouse of
knowledge. Trevor not only read and commented upon the entire
manuscript but also gave me a full afternoon's tutorial in
Bloomsbury, which made me recast several chunks of text.

Ann has remained as ever supportive as well as an ocean of calm
whenever I have had computing difficulties or the recurrent problem
of mislaid books, notes, and phrases. I owe much to her love and care.

Martyn Rady

Ramsgate
June 2016

List of illustrations

List of maps

Chapter 1
Dynasties and empires; titles and peoples

The Habsburgs: origins and name

After the house of Windsor, the Habsburgs are the best-known dynasty in Europe. Their history is tied up with most European countries. Habsburgs were at one time or other rulers of what are now Spain and Portugal, Belgium, Luxembourg, and the Netherlands, Germany, Austria, Hungary, Bosnia and Croatia, the Czech Republic (previously Bohemia and Moravia), Slovakia and Slovenia, as well as parts of Italy, Poland, Romania, Moldova, Serbia, and Ukraine. Their geographical sway in Europe has only been rivalled by the far more fleeting creations of Napoleon and Hitler. Further afield, their rule as kings of Spain reached to the New World, taking in much of Latin America and parts of the United States coastline. In the late 16th and 17th centuries, Habsburg power extended across the Pacific to include the Philippines. The Habsburgs might even have taken a part of the Arctic Archipelago, but the Austrian explorers who in 1872 first mapped the landscape just 500 miles from the North Pole only gave the territory a name, not claiming it for their ruler. Nevertheless, a part of northern Russia is still called Franz Josef Land, in memory of Emperor Franz Joseph (1848–1916), who despite his long service as monarch never settled whether his name should end with a 'ph' or an 'f'.

The Habsburgs ruled not only an extensive territory but did so for a long time. They were Europe's premier dynasty for almost half a millennium, from the 15th to the 20th century. The great moments and events of European history are indissolubly bound up with their name—from the confrontation with Luther that set the Reformation in motion to the victory at Blenheim over Louis XIV, to the vanquishing of Napoleon and, onwards, to the fatal decision taken in 1914 to embark on a European war. The pantheon of Habsburg rulers includes adventurers, lunatics, and at least one monarch who was so physically disfashioned that his true portrait could never be exhibited.

The Habsburgs retain a romantic allure and reputation for tragedy. Contemporaries were as much interested, however, in the history of Habsburg physiognomy and of the protruding jaw that belonged to Franz Joseph's ancestors. The deformity known as prognathism had by the mid-18th century largely worked its way out of the family's genetics. Even so, it long remained a source of speculation for eugenicists and theorists of degeneration, inspiring even in Franz Joseph's lifetime such works, embellished with the likenesses of the emperor's forebears, as *The Hereditability of Marks of Decrepitude in Sovereign Houses* and *A Study on the Inheritance of Maxillary Anomalies and Teeth*.

As far back as we can trace, the Habsburg family was illustrious. In the 10th century, its progenitors carved out a medley of discontinuous lordships and manors in the region of the Upper Rhine, ranging across Alsace, the Black Forest, and what is now northern Switzerland. Around 1030, the earliest Habsburg of whom we have a definite record, Radbot (*c*.985–1045), founded the Benedictine abbey at Muri in the Swiss Aargau. Muri served over several centuries as the family's place of burial. About the same time, Radbot built a stone fort called Habsburg some 30 kilometres away from Muri. The name probably means Castle by the Ford, but is usually given the grander rendering of Castle of the Hawk. It was by the title of Habsburg that Radbot's descendants were generally known.

Castle Habsburg was for several centuries the principal seat of the family. The territorial interests of the Habsburgs shifted, however, first northwards to Alsace and Swabia, and then in the second half of the 13th century eastwards, to the duchies of Austria and Styria. The reorientation of Habsburg interests led to the abandonment of Castle Habsburg. The fort was in 1230 given away to vassals, and then eventually lost. Much of what remained of the Habsburg properties in modern-day Switzerland was abandoned at the start of the next century, falling victim to the rebellion of the Swiss Confederates launched in legend by William Tell. Castle Habsburg survives, however, to this day, its main keep still standing, next to a restaurant, with parasols on the battlements. A little museum celebrates the castle's links to the Habsburgs, severed almost eight centuries ago.

During the 14th century, the Habsburgs abandoned their former name, assuming instead the description of House of Austria. Over time the old name of Habsburg acquired an almost pejorative meaning, recollecting a superseded and provincial past. When, therefore, around 1415 the Emperor Sigismund addressed Duke Ernest of Austria by the title 'Lord of Habsburg', the duke took offence and responded by calling the emperor 'Lord of Luxemburg'. It was only in the early 19th century that the name of Habsburg entered into common currency, partly as a consequence of Schiller's popular historical ballad, 'The Count of Habsburg' (1803). In English usage, however, the convention was until shortly after the First World War to spell Habsburg not in the German form but with a 'p'—hence 'Hapsburg'. This practice lasted longer in North America, but the German spelling is today generally preferred.

Empire and empires

Julius Caesar bequeathed his nickname to posterity. On account of his baldness contemporaries called Julius by way of a joke *Caesar* or 'hairy'. The soubriquet endured as a title of majesty. Kaiser,

Tsar, and Kayser-i Rum (a title of the Ottoman sultans) have their origin in the name of Caesar and in the ambition of the earliest bearers of the title to match the Roman Empire of classical antiquity. The Middle Ages saw a proliferation of Caesars and self-styled empires on Europe's fringe—in Byzantium and in its cultural satellites of Bulgaria and Serbia, and at the end of the 15th century in Muscovite Russia. Their adoption of Roman greatness was considered risible in most of Europe. In western Christendom there was until the time of Napoleon only one true empire—the Holy Roman Empire.

The Holy Roman Empire had its origin on Christmas Day, AD 800, with the pope's coronation in Rome of Charlemagne, king of the Franks, as emperor of the Romans. The Empire languished under Charlemagne's successors, but was revived in the mid-10th century as an 'East Frankish' and increasingly German institution. The Holy Roman Empire was initially conceived both as the direct successor to the old Roman Empire and as the secular counterpart to the spiritual empire of the popes. But the rulers of Europe's kingdoms resented the sovereignty claimed by the emperors. The reach of the Holy Roman Emperor was thus confined to the broad swathe of territories which reached from the Baltic Sea to the Mediterranean—to what are now Germany and the Low Countries, Switzerland, Austria, Slovenia, the Czech Republic, northern Italy, and part of Poland.

From the very first, the emperors had to negotiate with the princes of the Holy Roman Empire, who built up their own territories within its borders, pursuing their own policies and interests. It is a mark of the princes' power that they had the right to elect the emperor. Despite the electoral character of the imperial office, emperors once in office could use their influence to ensure that their sons were voted as their successors, even in their own lifetime. From 1438 to 1740 all the Holy Roman Emperors were Habsburgs. The line expired on the death of Emperor Charles VI, who only had a daughter, Maria Theresa, on which account the electors chose a Bavarian prince as Charles's successor. On his death in 1745, the electors chose as emperor the husband of Maria Theresa, Duke Francis of Lorraine. In this roundabout way the imperial crown once more returned to the Habsburgs.

The first Holy Roman Emperors were indeed crowned in Rome, but on account of the costs and dangers of the journey coronation by the pope became infrequent. The last emperor to be crowned by the pope in Rome was Frederick III, in 1452. Instead, the rulers of the Holy Roman Empire made do with a coronation as 'king of the Romans' in the chapel of Charlemagne's old palace in Aachen (later in Frankfurt Cathedral), which gave them full rights as emperor. With the pope's agreement, King Maximilian of Habsburg assumed in 1508 the title 'by the Grace of God elected Emperor of the Romans', which became the description used by his successors. The title of 'king of the Romans' was henceforth mainly reserved for any heir-apparent who might be elected in advance of the reigning emperor's death.

In its symbolism alone, Napoleon's coronation in 1804 as emperor of the French, in the presence of the pope, indicated that the days of the Holy Roman Empire were numbered. Anticipating its end, the Holy Roman Emperor, Francis II, declared himself emperor of Austria. Although Francis was often portrayed in coronation robes and wearing a crown taken from the Habsburg treasury, he was not formally crowned as emperor of Austria. None of Francis's heirs were crowned either—they simply assumed power by proclamation on the death or abdication of their predecessor.

For two years, Francis was both Holy Roman Emperor and emperor of Austria. Threatened by Napoleon with immediate war unless he complied, Francis announced in 1806 the abolition of the Holy Roman Empire and his own abdication as its ruler. The document of abdication and of imperial dissolution rehearsed Francis's titles and honours, even including the designation 'At all times Enlarger of the Empire'. From this year onwards, the Habsburg rulers counted themselves only as emperors of Austria. So Francis II became Francis I; his successor became Ferdinand I (rather than Ferdinand V), and so on. As a mark of continuity, however, the double-headed eagle, a symbol of imperial majesty since the 15th century, was included on the arms of the new Austrian Empire.

After Napoleon's defeat, most of the German lands were reorganized as the German Confederation—a loose political association which became the German Empire in 1871. The Habsburgs retained the territories to the east and south of the new Germany, becoming now an exclusively Central European entity. After 1867, the portion of the Habsburg Empire occupied by the kingdom of Hungary received home rule. Thereafter, the Habsburg Empire was also known as the Austro-Hungarian Empire, Austria-Hungary, or Dual Monarchy (but never Dual Empire). From an overall population of 30 million in 1800, it had grown by 1910 to 50 million persons, making it the third most populous state in Europe after Russia and Germany.

The 19th century witnessed therefore a multiplication of empires in Europe—French, German, and Austrian. Before this time, however, there was in most of Europe only one empire, the Holy Roman Empire, over which an emperor drawn from the Habsburg family generally presided.

Collecting crowns

The Habsburg possessions reached far beyond the confines of the Holy Roman Empire. On occasions, we may spot some slippage, whereby the name of 'empire' was applied to the possessions over which the Habsburgs ruled. More usually, the Habsburgs referred to the territories over which they ruled as a *monarchia* or 'monarchy' or, even more simply, as 'our lands'.

The *monarchia* of the Habsburgs was built up over centuries and was subject to major alterations. Its core was from the late 13th century roughly coterminous with modern-day Austria and Slovenia, reaching southwards to the Adriatic coast. This area consisted of a medley of duchies and minor principalities which the Habsburgs governed as hereditary dukes and counts—Upper and Lower Austria, the Tyrol, Styria, Carinthia, Carniola, Vorarlberg, Görz-Gradisca, and Trieste. They also continued to rule over the patchwork of lordships and counties in Alsace and around the Upper Rhine which had previously formed the basis of their power. These possessions together with portions of land in the duchy of Swabia which they obtained in the 13th century were known as 'Further Austria'.

In 1477, the son of Emperor Frederick III, Maximilian, acquired by marriage and not a little force the rump of the duchy of Burgundy, which brought with it the Low Countries and the wealth of their maritime cities, as well as the little territorial enclave of Charolais in France. Maximilian, who became Holy Roman Emperor in 1508, pursued the risky policy of making marriages between his family and the leading royal houses of Europe. These might easily have come unstuck, with the consequence that the possessions of the Habsburgs passed to others.

Fortune, however, favoured Maximilian. In 1496–7, Maximilian's son and daughter, Philip the Handsome and Margaret of Austria, married into the line of the Spanish rulers of Castile and Aragon. Margaret's marriage did not endure, her husband soon dying heirless, but Philip's union to Juana the Mad (*La Loca*, so called because she was) prospered, and in 1506 he inherited through her the crown of Castile. Ten years later, Philip's son, Charles, succeeded as Castile's king, to which the neighbouring kingdom of Aragon was now added. Along with the Spanish inheritance came Naples and southern Italy, Sicily and Sardinia, settlements on the North African coast, and the Spanish possessions in the New World.

The Habsburg Empire

Frederick III
Holy Roman Emperor (1452–93)

Maximilian I *m.* Mary of Burgundy
Holy Roman Emperor (1508–19)

Philip the Handsome
King of Castile (1506)
m. Juana the Mad of Castile

Margaret of Austria
m. Juan of Castile

Charles V
Holy Roman Emperor (1519–58),
King of Spain
m. Isabella of Portugal

Ferdinand I
Holy Roman Emperor (1558–64)
m. Anne of Jagiello

Mary (of Hungary)
m. Louis II Jagiello (dies 1526)
King of Bohemia and Hungary

Philip II of Spain
(1556–98)

Maximilian II
Holy Roman Emperor
(1564–76)

Ferdinand
of the Tyrol

Charles of Styria

SPANISH LINE

CENTRAL EUROPEAN LINE

1. The branches of the Habsburg family in the sixteenth century.

8

Charles subsequently succeeded Maximilian by election as Holy Roman Emperor in 1519, becoming Emperor Charles V.

Meanwhile, Charles's younger brother, Ferdinand, for whom Maximilian had engineered marriage into the Polish Jagiello line, acquired in 1526 the crowns of Hungary and Bohemia, following the death in battle of his Jagiello brother-in-law, Louis. In the space of just half a century, therefore, the two Habsburg brothers, Charles and Ferdinand, had through Maximilian's marriage schemes taken over half of Europe, and they had done so more or less peacefully. Only in Hungary was there any concerted resistance. As an adage put it at the time, 'Let others fight, you Happy Austria marry.'

There were thus two main branches of the Habsburgs after 1526. First, there was the 'Spanish' line that descended from Charles V and which brought together Spain, the Low Countries, parts of Italy, and the New World. Between 1580 and 1640, the Spanish Habsburgs also ruled Portugal and thus had possession of the Portuguese colony of Brazil and the outposts of Goa in southern India, Macau on the Chinese coast, and a small part of the city of Nagasaki in Japan. Secondly, there was the 'Central European' line that originated with Ferdinand and had as its core the Austrian lands, Bohemia, and Hungary. The office of Holy Roman Emperor, although elective, was by agreement between Charles and Ferdinand vested in the Central European line (Map 1).

All of the Habsburg possessions were 'composite' states and kingdoms, comprising several or more territories which had over time become bound together under single rulers. Aragon thus consisted of three parts: Aragon itself, Valencia, and Catalonia, as well as its possessions in the Mediterranean, including the kingdoms of Naples and Sicily (known collectively as the Two Sicilies). The Low Countries comprised a patchwork of principalities, some of which were until 1549 considered parts of France. Bohemia included Bohemia itself, with its capital

9

The Habsburg Empire

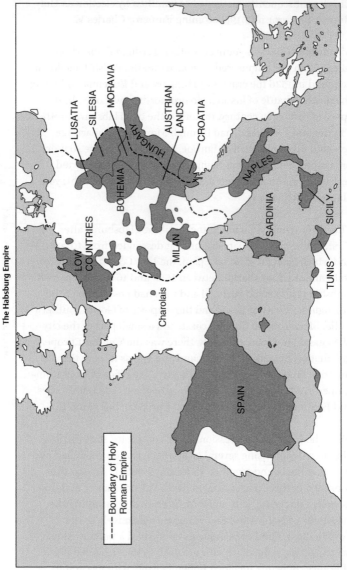

Map 1. Habsburg possessions in Europe c.1560.

LUSATIA
SILESIA
MORAVIA
AUSTRIAN LANDS
CROATIA
HUNGARY
BOHEMIA
NAPLES
SARDINIA
SICILY
LOW COUNTRIES
MILAN
TUNIS
Charolais
SPAIN

- - - - Boundary of Holy Roman Empire

in Prague, Moravia, Silesia, and Lusatia, which was further divided into two parts. Silesia is now mostly in Poland, and Lusatia is split between Poland and Germany. Hungary comprised two kingdoms, Hungary and Croatia, although there was only a single coronation, and the partly self-governing provinces of Transylvania and Slavonia. The lands belonging to Ferdinand's heirs were much later augmented by territories taken from Poland and by the duchies of northern Italy. Maria Theresa's marriage to Francis of Lorraine brought with it the empty title of king of Jerusalem, which also belonged, again in name alone, to the Spanish branch of the family.

The complexity of the territories over which the two branches of the family ruled is demonstrated by their formal styles, given in Box 1. The *etcetera* at the end of each indicates that there were

Box 1 Titles of the two branches

The titles of Philip IV (1648): Don Philip IV, by the Grace of God King of Castile, León, Aragon, the Two Sicilies, Jerusalem, Portugal, Navarre, Granada, Toledo, Valencia, Galicia, Majorca, Minorca, Seville, Sardinia, Cordoba, Corsica, Murcia, Jaén, the Algarves, Algeciras, Gibraltar, the Canary Islands, the East and West Indies, the islands and mainlands of the Ocean, Archduke of Austria, Lord of Burgundy, Brabant and Milan, Count of Habsburg, Flanders, Tyrol, Barcelona, Seigneur of Vizcaya, Molina etc.

The titles of Ferdinand III (1648): Ferdinand III, Elected Roman Emperor, at all times Enlarger of the Empire, King of Germany, Hungary, Bohemia, Dalmatia, Croatia, Slavonia etc, Archduke of Austria, Duke of Burgundy, Brabant, Styria, Carinthia, Carniola, Margrave of Moravia, Duke of Luxembourg, Upper and Lower Silesia, Württemberg and Teck, Prince in Swabia, Count of Habsburg, Tyrol, Kyburg, Gorizia, Landgrave of Alsace, Margrave of the Holy Roman Empire, Burgau, Upper and Lower Lusatia, Lord of the Windisch Mark, Pordenone and Salins etc.

additional titles that could have been included. Indeed, over time more and more were added, including possessions and properties which had only ever briefly, and in some cases never, belonged to their predecessors. By having these places listed, they were kept 'active', as possible future acquisitions should the right circumstances arise.

Dynasty and subjects

The Habsburgs were not just a ruling family. They were also a dynasty. A dynasty is more than a group of blood relatives, for it has a sense of its own history that guides its development through time. It is proprietary, in the sense of seeking to retain and even augment its landed inheritance, but it is also a legal community, whose members have interconnected rights and obligations. With the passage of generations, a dynasty may acquire a set of customs and beliefs about itself, which serves to cement a common identity and purpose.

The Habsburg dynasty was all of these things. It held to a mythologized history that taught it to expect greatness. It was tenacious in acquiring lands, kingdoms, and titles, either by war or by marriage. Its members were, moreover, bound together both biologically and by the distribution of power and honours. The branches of the dynasty thus regularly intermarried, to such an extent that Charles II of Spain (1665–1700) had only two-thirds the normal number of great- and great-great-grandparents. Inbreeding between cousins and uncles caused the prognathism for which the Habsburgs were famous and was most pronounced in Charles II (Figure 2).

Within the dynasty, lands and kingdoms were frequently divided up among heirs, which fostered a sense of political partnership. It was only with the Pragmatic Sanction of 1713, which laid down the principle of primogeniture, that partition among male heirs was abandoned. Before this time, succession to titles was often

2. Charles II of Spain by Juan Carreño de Miranda, 1685. Inbreeding not only caused the deformation of the jaw but also left the king mentally disabled.

decided by 'house agreements' which distributed the dynasty's lands among family members as if they were private property. Those left out of these arrangements were often given governorships. The Habsburgs were striking in the way that they used daughters not only as political pawns but also as political players, administering parts of the dynasty's possessions.

Dynastic ambition was only one factor that guided the Habsburg rulers. Indeed, on occasions the policies they pursued were potentially damaging and even ruinous to the dynasty's interests and survival. These other guiding principles and determinants of policy included the conviction that as Holy Roman Emperors the Habsburg rulers had an obligation to defend the Catholic Church and to promote its spiritual interests, which included the promotion of peace. They also embraced the belief that government was a trust and that rulership implied duties to subjects. Although rarely doubting the divine providence that vindicated their power and ordained the secular hierarchy on which they stood at the apex, the Habsburg emperors took their obligations to their subjects seriously. Right through to the 20th century, their mornings were typically occupied by audiences at which up to a hundred petitioners queued to ask the sovereign for his help or advice, or (which was more usual) to thank him in person for some kindness shown.

There were two problems with the cultivation of good government. The first was the problem of distance, which meant that Habsburg rulers might demonstrate their personal rule and fatherly concern only to a few. Country folk from Lower Austria might thus travel to Vienna to have a private word with the emperor about their daughters' marriages, but this was scarcely possible for most Habsburg subjects. The old adage of Spanish colonial rule, 'If death came from Madrid, we would be immortal', was a fitting verdict on the problems of communication that beset Habsburg rule more generally. It did not help that so many Habsburg rulers understood good government to be synonymous with efficient bureaucracy. After a little travelling, usually at the outset of their reigns, they sheltered in the Escorial palace outside Madrid or the Hofburg in Vienna, drafting instructions, commenting on ministerial advice, and reading military dispatches. Huge swathes of their territories went unvisited, in some cases for centuries. Hungary was particularly neglected, imperial travel there being mostly confined to brisk dashes across the Hungarian border to the castle at Bratislava (called Pressburg in German, and Pozsony in Hungarian).

Government thus operated at a distance and through representatives of the ruler—viceroys, governors, and executive councils. In each of the territories to which they were appointed, these agents confronted local nobilities, whose hereditary privileges and rights were as historically grounded as the authority claimed by the Habsburgs, and often older. For every land, petty county, duchy, and kingdom that the Habsburgs ruled, there was a corresponding territorial nobility. Each group of noblemen claimed special liberties to go with their rank and each lived by its own laws and customs. These, so they maintained, were not dependent on the ruler's consent or gift, but were separately generated. The nobilities typically demanded the right to be consulted in all matters of importance affecting the territory in which they lived, particularly when it involved the raising of revenues or the recruitment of troops. Their parliaments, or diets as they were known, were frequently at odds with the ruler. The diets of Hungary and Bohemia also alleged the right to elect their monarchs. The Habsburgs might treat their possessions after the manner of private property, but their Bohemian and Hungarian subjects believed that they might still choose who ruled over them.

Power relations on the ground were thus characterized by what has been called 'structural dualism'. On the one side, there was the ruler and his agents; on the other, the nobility, which claimed an equal voice in much of business of government. This was frustrating and so it is not surprising that the Habsburgs whittled away at noble privileges and tried to make the diets more pliable. Where in addition to noblemen the diets included representatives drawn from the towns, clergy, and better-off peasantry, then they might practise a policy of 'divide and rule'. Or they might simply ignore the diets, not bothering to institute laws by consent, but instead issuing decrees and enforcing their will through the deployment of commissars backed up by troops.

Below the nobility were the peasantry. Their condition varied from place to place. Nonetheless, 19th-century Austrian statisticians arrived at a rough scheme, based on a west–east 'cultural gradient', which almost worked. By this measure, the further east one went the more economically depressed and culturally impoverished the population. The Austrian lands and Further Austria were wealthy, sustained by cities, commerce, mineral extraction, and a largely emancipated peasantry, for whose farms the peasants paid rents to their landlords and were not obliged to perform onerous labour services. Further east, however, the cities shrank in size, became fewer, and the population thinned out. The demands of landlords were accordingly greater, as they needed a servile workforce to till their own estates.

The nobility who dominated the countryside extracted during the 17th and 18th centuries increasingly burdensome dues from their peasants. Relations between noble lords and their tenants were long regarded as private matters, in which government should not interfere. Nevertheless, from the very first the Habsburg rulers used their officials to clamp down on manifest injustices. In the 18th century, they actively promoted the interests of the peasantry, putting an upper limit on rents and labour obligations. For the Habsburgs, the benefits of good government were not reserved to the privileged orders. As Leopold II (1790–2) explained, 'Princes must always be conscious . . . that they owe their position only to an agreement between other men; that they in turn must perform all their duties and tasks, as rightly expected of them . . . Princes must always consider that they cannot degrade other men without degrading themselves.' The Empress Maria Theresa (1740–80) put it more simply when she called herself 'chief mother of my country'.

The territories over which the Habsburgs ruled differed over time, as did their titles. The dynasty's goals and ambitions also changed, from crown-collecting to the championing of the Catholic faith, and from the defence of Europe against the Turks to the struggle against the tide of revolutionary republicanism. In this book, we will explore these changes of ambition, fortune, and mission.

Chapter 2
The imperial vision: 11th to 16th century

Medieval ambitions

Most medieval forgeries were done well. Genuine charters were
copied, insertions carefully made into their texts, and seals
appended that had been taken from elsewhere. Historians continue
to be caught out by them. What follows is, by contrast, an obvious
deception. Drawn up in 1358 under the direction of Duke Rudolf IV
of Habsburg, it purports to be a charter issued by Julius Caesar.

> We Emperor Julius, Caesar and Worshipper of the gods, Supreme
> Augustus of the imperial land, Strengthener of the whole universe,
> to Austria and its people, the grace of Rome and our peace. We
> order you to obey the lofty senator, our uncle, since upon our victory
> we have given you to him and to his heirs and house, to be his and
> his posterity's possession in fief for always, and we will ordain no
> power over him. We give to him and his successors all the fruits of
> Austria; moreover, we promote our uncle and his successors to
> membership of the innermost council of Rome, so that from now
> on no weighty business or matter may be resolved without his
> knowledge. Given in Rome, capital of the world, on the Day of
> Venus, in the first year of our reign...

Even at the time, Julius's charter was regarded as fraudulent
on account of its clumsy Latin and anachronistic content.

Nevertheless, it was from the 14th century onwards used to buttress the claims of the house of Habsburg to pre-eminence in the Holy Roman Empire. By virtue of this and other similar deceptions (including a charter purportedly written by the Roman emperor, Nero), the Habsburgs 'discovered' that they were entitled to the rank of archduke. It was by this spoof title that all senior members of the dynasty subsequently styled themselves, in honour of which they wore a cloak trimmed with ermine and a coronet.

The story behind the forgeries rests on politics and ambition. In the 11th and 12th centuries, Radbot and the first Habsburgs had sought to carve out a principality in the region of Switzerland and the Upper Rhine. They were, however, unable to consolidate their disparate properties into a unified block, for the region was intersected by too many rival lordships, cities, and confederacies. One thing the early Habsburgs did have was money, for they controlled the Alpine toll stations which stood between the upland pastures and the cities of the valleys. In the hope that his family's wealth might be deployed to bring order to the Holy Roman Empire, the German princes elected Rudolf of Habsburg as king in 1273. He did not disappoint them, deploying his armies against the robber-knights whose Rhineland castles impeded merchants and commerce.

Had he bothered to seek coronation in Rome, Rudolf I might have become emperor. His principal interest was, however, in the contested duchies of Austria and Styria. These had belonged to the Babenberg family which had become extinct in the 1240s and whose lands had been seized by the Czech king, Ottokar of Bohemia. Rudolf appealed to the leading lords of the Empire and received their support to bring Ottokar to heel. In August 1278, Ottokar's forces were defeated and the Bohemian king was slain.

Rudolf's capture of the eastern duchies transformed the basis of Habsburg power, giving Rudolf and his descendants a compact and wealthy body of land. Rudolf's successors went on to take the neighbouring duchies of Vorarlberg, Carinthia, and Carniola, to which they later added the adjacent city of Trieste and the County of Görz-Gradisca. Other families, however, succeeded to the title of king and emperor. Like the Habsburgs, the Luxemburg family vied for Ottokar's inheritance and it had married into the dead king's line, thereby acquiring the Bohemian crown. In 1356, Emperor Charles IV of Luxemburg published the so-called Golden Bull (such was its importance that it carried a golden *bulla* or seal), which listed the seven princes who were entitled to elect any future ruler. The Habsburgs were conspicuously omitted. It was to make up for this slight that Rudolf IV engaged in his work of falsification, giving his predecessors a pedigree that went back to classical Rome. Whereas others might hold their rank of a modern emperor's will, the dignity of the Habsburgs was rooted in Julius Caesar's.

Rudolf IV not only forged. Known to history as 'the founder', he sought to make Vienna the physical symbol of Habsburg greatness and a rival to Emperor Charles IV's seat in Prague. He established a university and built the great choir of St Stephen's Church in Vienna. Although Vienna only received its first bishop in 1469, it was important to Rudolf that the city should look as if it had a cathedral. Likewise, because saints added lustre to a dynasty but the Habsburgs were short of these, Rudolf pressed the pope to canonize the 12th-century Austrian ruler, Leopold the Good. Although Leopold belonged to the extinct Babenberg line and was not a Habsburg, Rudolf presented Leopold as a direct forebear, in whose honour successive archdukes were named.

Rudolf's ambition for his family was also demonstrated in the inheritance pact that he made with the widowed countess of the Tyrol. According to its terms, if the line of either expired through lack of heirs, the other would succeed to their properties. So when the countess died in 1369, her son having predeceased her, Rudolf took the Tyrol (although he had to fight to keep it), thus creating a link between his Austrian lands and the remaining Habsburg possessions to the west.

Rudolf IV died young, still in his mid-twenties. As Rudolf had no son, his brothers divided his inheritance, which was then further partitioned among their heirs. The fortunes of biology saved the Habsburgs from the territorial attrition of partible inheritance. In 1437, the Emperor Sigismund, son of Charles IV of Luxemburg, died without heir. Meanwhile, the various cadet lines of the Habsburgs either expired or faltered, leaving children as heirs. In 1438, the electors chose as king Albert of Habsburg, the late Emperor Sigismund's son-in-law. Upon Albert's death the next year, they appointed as successor his second cousin, Frederick of Styria, who was now the senior member of the dynasty.

Frederick was chosen by the electors because there was no one else available for the role of king. Nevertheless, he looked the part, for he was tall and muscular, with long blond hair—characteristics that he had inherited from his Polish mother, Cymburga, a woman of prodigious beauty and physical strength, who could reputedly drive nails into oak tables with her bare fist. Frederick ruled as king of Germany from 1440 and, following his coronation in Rome, as emperor from 1452 until his death in 1493.

AEIOU

Historians have not looked kindly upon Frederick III, too readily following the later description of him as the 'arch-sleepyhead' or averring by reference to the Austrian poet Rilke that his main achievement was to have reigned in adversity for so long: 'Who speaks of victory, when to endure is all?' An even harsher verdict blames Frederick for Germany's later misfortunes. Instead of busying himself with the Holy Roman Empire and trying to bring order to its politics, Frederick withdrew to provincial Wiener Neustadt and occupied himself with Habsburg family affairs. For a quarter of a century, he did not leave the Austrian lands. The opportunity to recast the Empire into a modern, centralized state was thus lost.

Frederick was, however, aware that to rule the Holy Roman Empire effectively he needed a strong territorial base. The office of king and emperor brought little by way of material reward and the imperial diet seldom agreed to the tax demands that rulers set before it. Much of Frederick's reign was thus spent recovering the lands which had been inherited by other branches of the family. In warfare mostly unsuccessful, Frederick obtained his purpose by underhand diplomacy and by simply outliving his kinsmen. Even so, at the end of his reign he was driven out of Lower Austria and Vienna by his adversary, the king of Hungary.

For Frederick, there was no distinction between a policy aimed at enlarging his family's interests and one intended to benefit the Holy Roman Empire. The two were not only mutually reinforcing but also interwoven. At his instruction, chroniclers and genealogists wrote new histories that showed the interrelationship of the Habsburgs to the main themes and personalities of the imperial past, going back to the classical period and even to the Old Testament. Most of these histories were a reworking of a late 14th-century text, known as the *Chronicle of the Ninety-Five Lords*, which related the generations of the princes who 'from the time before Christ have ruled Austria', interspersing their biographies with sketches of Roman rulers and emperors. Frederick held this chronicle in such affection that he had the east wall of St George's Cathedral in Wiener Neustadt adorned with the requisite number of coats of arms. Among these were placed angels who bore his symbol, the acrostic AEIOU. Although capable of many readings—several hundred or more are suspected—the dominant meaning was *Austria Est Imperator Orbis Universae*: 'Austria is Emperor of the Whole World'.

Historians continue to deride Frederick III's AEIOU acrostic as being as empty of substance as the forgeries of Rudolf IV. It is not, however, entirely inappropriate as his epitaph. Back in the late 1430s, it was still difficult to imagine that the Habsburgs might become lasting rulers of the Holy Roman Empire. By the time of Frederick's death, it was hard to conceive of any other dynasty holding the office of emperor. By endurance alone, Frederick III had made the Habsburgs an imperial dynasty.

Frederick's son, Maximilian, was elected as his heir and co-ruler in 1486 and he moved effortlessly into power upon his father's death seven years later. The itinerary of his travels marks him out as quite different from his father, for he was always on the move, scarcely staying more than a few weeks in any one place. This was not on account of restlessness. Maximilian's style of rule depended on personality and presence and, since he could not be everywhere at once, on the projection of his image. Several thousand surviving portraits attest to Maximilian's determination to make his face the best known in Europe. Artists were enlisted to communicate his image and achievements in yet more dramatic ways. Albrecht Dürer, Albrecht Altdorfer, and a team of less well-known engravers designed for him the two massive woodcut series, the 'Triumphal Procession' and the 'Triumphal Gate', which advertised Maximilian's ancestry and accomplishments. Made up of interlocking printed sheets, they were intended to be pasted up as wallpaper in halls and palaces.

Maximilian was active in his own self-fashioning. He oversaw the composition of two allegorical autobiographies in which he depicted himself as the chivalric 'White King' (*Weisskunig*), bent on knight-errantry, damsel-rescue, and crusade. Maximilian's forays into history and genealogy were equally fantastic. At a time when most rulers were content to trace their descent to the Trojans, Maximilian worked even further back, to Noah, and he bullied the Theology Faculty of Vienna University to confirm his Old Testament ancestry. (To go any further back than Noah was pointless, for we are all the descendants of Adam and Eve.) He also built outwards, linking his family tree by marriage and kinship to prophets, Greek and Egyptian demi-gods, one hundred popes, saints, and martyrs, and all the ruling houses of Europe.

All of this might be considered megalomania, except that Maximilian's imaginings resonated in his own actions. In 1477, following the defeat and death of Duke Charles of Burgundy, Maximilian hastened to the defence of Charles's daughter, Mary. After staged battles with rivals for Mary's hand, he married her and grabbed the lion's share of her inheritance; the rest was seized by France. He then fought the French for possession of Milan and, subsequently, campaigned against Venice.

Promotion of his dynasty inspired not only genealogical fancy but also Maximilian's marriage schemes with the ruling house of Spain and with the Jagiello king of Hungary and Bohemia. Bernhard Strigel's portrait of Maximilian and his family (Figure 3), which was composed around 1516 celebrated Maximilian's designs and anticipated their fulfilment. Intended to mark the betrothal of the Jagiello prince, Louis, to Maximilian's granddaughter, Mary, Strigel presented Louis as a member of Maximilian's family. Louis's death ten years later would give Maximilian's grandson Ferdinand, depicted by Strigel as cuddling the old emperor's arm, the opportunity to succeed Louis as king of Hungary and Bohemia and to win Central Europe for the Habsburgs.

Within the Empire there was widespread concern that Maximilian would use his authority to extract troops and cash from the princes and cities in order to advance his own private interests. Plainly, though, some reform was needed, both to preserve peace within the Empire's frontiers and to meet the growing Ottoman Turkish threat in the east. Plans to establish a government appointed by the imperial diet and to establish new organs of justice for the adjudication of disputes faltered, mostly on account of Maximilian's opposition. No new governmental institutions were established nor a reformed system of tax collection,

3. Family of Maximilian I by Bernhard Strigel, 1516. Top row: Maximilian I, Philip the Handsome, and Mary of Burgundy. Bottom row: the future monarchs, Ferdinand I, Charles V, and Louis II of Hungary. The family portrait is a work of imagination. Mary looks towards heaven precisely because she had long departed this life, in 1482. Philip died in 1506. Charles and Ferdinand were brought up separately, in the Low Countries and Castile respectively, and met for the first time only in 1517.

although, perversely, two rival high courts were founded with overlapping jurisdictions—one appointed by the diet and one presided over by the emperor. In the absence of a strong centre, real power continued to be exercised by the local princes and regional groupings of lords and cities, which increasingly took over the task of maintaining the peace. The Holy Roman Empire thus entered the modern period in much the same form it had inherited from the Middle Ages—as a loose association of fragmented territories, bound together by a name and by nominal allegiance to a single ruler.

Charles V and Spain

Strigel's portrait shows in the centre the future emperor and king of Spain, Charles—an unimposing youth whose mouth, as in the picture, permanently gaped. The young man entered upon his Spanish inheritance in 1516 as the heir to the Spanish crowns via his father's marriage to Juana, the daughter and only surviving child of Isabella of Castile and Ferdinand of Aragon. His Spanish possessions included Sicily and southern Italy and Sardinia, augmented between 1510 and 1520 by enclaves on the North African coast and, later, by Tunis. It was also during Charles's reign as king of Spain that much of the New World became Spanish—Mexico after 1519, and the former Inca Empire, centred upon Peru, after 1529. An expedition from the Spanish Caribbean island of Hispaniola (now shared by the Dominican Republic and Haiti) founded in 1526 the first named settlement on the territory of what would become the United States, on the coast of today's state of Georgia. Further afield, the Philippines were claimed for Spain by the explorer Magellan in 1521, later being named in honour of Charles's son.

Shortly after Charles arrived in Spain for the first time there was a revolt against his rule, occasioned in the main by the avarice of his Burgundian courtiers who had started to pillage Spanish revenues. The rebellion was put down but Charles learned from it.

Hereafter, his preferred method of rule, both in Spain and elsewhere, was to work in collaboration with the existing power-holders and elites, deferring to their privileges and seeking to achieve consensus. Although he did not generally entrust Spanish aristocratic grandees with a share in the practical work of government, he gave them military commands and viceroyalties abroad. He also admitted them to the Order of the Golden Fleece, an originally Burgundian chivalric society, whose members were at its meetings able to treat with the monarch on equal terms.

Charles's preference for negotiation was most apparent in his dealings with the Castilian and Aragonese parliaments. He met with the Castilian parliament, the Cortes, roughly every three years, and with its Aragonese equivalent, the Corts General, about every five. Charles never submitted to the principle that Spain's parliaments should only grant the ruler new taxes in return for him agreeing to their demands. Nevertheless, by hearing petitions of the Cortes and Corts General, and often enacting them as law, Charles reinforced the idea that there was a contract between monarch and subjects, and that the royal power was not unlimited but to some degree constitutionally constrained.

Charles made a political virtue out of financial exigency. He needed money. In Castile he had the right as monarch to collect a range of taxes, without the consent of the Cortes. These were always the first revenues to be allocated to support his ventures or to be offered up as collateral on loans. After that, he depended on special votes of money by the Cortes, which meant that it had to be summoned. By the 1530s the Cortes of Castile was protesting that the wealth of the kingdom was exhausted and too much misspent abroad, and it resisted Charles's demand for additional taxes. By this time, however, Charles had access to fresh funds, in the form of the revenues of the New World, to which were soon added the profits of the Bolivian silver mines. Even so, the sums obtained from Spain and the New World were insufficient and Charles was obliged to borrow from German and Italian bankers, often at ruinous rates of interest. Although comparisons can be misleading, in respect of his principal adversaries Charles obtained from Spain and its overseas possessions a little under half the revenues available to the French king and less than a quarter of the Ottoman sultan's income.

Impecuniousness did not restrict Charles's ambition. As he explained to the Cortes of Castile in 1527, 'It is very pusillanimous for a prince to forgo undertaking a course of action merely because money is wanting, for in matters of honour a prince must not only risk his own person but also pledge the revenues of his treasury.' For half of his forty-year reign, Charles was at war with France, fighting in Italy, the Pyrenees, and along the western frontier of the Holy Roman Empire. He engaged the Ottomans on the Danube, led fleets against their North African allies, and campaigned throughout the Holy Roman Empire. 'Honour and reputation', the two watchwords of his Spanish predecessors, drove him forward—likewise his vain determination to recover the Burgundian lands lost to France in 1477, to make good his claims in Italy, where he succeeded, and to carry forward the fight against the enemies of the Church, in which he largely failed.

In reviewing the course of his life, Charles listed his travels to an audience in Brussels: 'I have been nine times to Germany, six times to Spain, and seven to Italy; I have come here to Flanders ten times, and have been four times to France in war and peace, twice to England, and twice to Africa... without mentioning other lesser journeys. I have made eight voyages in the Mediterranean and three in the seas of Spain...' The device that he bore as his personal emblem, the Pillars of Hercules with the motto *Plus Oultre* ('Still Further'), symbolized a reign spent mostly either on horseback or, on account of piles and gout, on a litter. But Charles was not a representative of the Middle Ages and a throwback to a bygone age, as once depicted by an older generation of historians. In Spain, he pursued a programme of institutional reform, building on the work of his predecessors but also borrowing Burgundian financial practices. Councils and committees, staffed by lawyers and skilled secretaries, who were often drawn from the lower nobility and cities, oversaw the business of government, preparing summaries of their discussions and making recommendations to him. Government was still small. In the localities and cities its writ barely ran, and in the turbulent kingdom of Aragon the royal will was frequently thwarted. It is, nonetheless, a mark of Charles's achievement as a harnesser of men and resources that he was able to do so much with relatively little.

The Empire divided

In 1519, Charles was elected in his absence Holy Roman Emperor and successor to his grandfather, Maximilian. Hastening to Germany, Charles was crowned king of the Romans in Aachen. Shortly afterwards, he presided over the meeting of the imperial diet at Worms. It was here that he met Martin Luther. Luther reiterated his controversial beliefs before the diet, and Charles confirmed them as heretical. The reasons that Charles gave were cogent—Luther considered the Church to have been in error for a thousand years, but it seemed to Charles more likely 'that a single monk must err if his opinion is contrary to all that of Christendom'. As Charles explained, his Spanish ancestors and imperial predecessors had been 'defenders at all times of the Catholic faith, its sacred ceremonies, decrees and ordinances, and its holy rites'. Charles thus had no other option than to condemn Luther as an outlaw and to forbid his teachings.

Following the diet, Charles returned to Spain. He appointed his brother, Ferdinand, as his regent in the Holy Roman Empire and assigned to him the Habsburg lands in Austria. Ferdinand was unable, however, to halt the spread of Luther's teachings and the Protestant Reformation which Luther had inspired. Although it would be more than two decades before a majority of the Empire's princes and great lords sided definitively with the Reformation, most adopted a tolerant position, not wishing to offend their vassals or inflame relations with the cities, where the new teaching established early footholds. More extreme varieties of the new faith also prospered. Often combining with apocalyptic teaching, they fed ideas of social revolution and contributed to the massive popular uprising in Germany in 1525, known as the Peasants' War. Ten years later, the city of Münster instituted a theocracy, under the rule of self-proclaimed prophets, to prepare for the end-times. The movement was crushed by Münster's bishop. The iron cages in which the corpses of the executed prophets were displayed still hang from Münster's cathedral walls.

Ferdinand had pressing problems of his own. In accordance with his grandfather's arrangements, in 1521 he had married Anne, the sister of King Louis of Hungary and Bohemia. The next year, Louis had married Ferdinand's sister, Mary, thus uniting the Habsburg and Jagiello families in a double marriage. In 1526, however, King Louis was killed by the Turks at the Battle of Mohács. Ferdinand moved swiftly to take Bohemia and Hungary for himself in the manner of a dowry, as his critics put it. In Hungary, however, the diet demanded the right to elect the dead king's successor, and it perversely appointed two kings—Ferdinand, and the leading Hungarian landowner, John Szapolyai (Zápolya), who promptly allied with the Turks. From this point onwards, Ferdinand seldom controlled more than a slice of Hungarian territory. In 1529, Ottoman forces broke through the Habsburg defences to put Vienna under siege. Ferdinand's concern for his Austrian possessions and for his claim to Hungary prevented him from taking a determined stand against the Reformation, for he needed a united imperial diet to vote him cash and troops. In his own possessions, however, he banned Lutheran preaching and forbade the distribution of Protestant literature.

Charles always maintained that he sought 'peace among Christians'. His hope was that negotiation and compromise might yield a solution to the religious impasse. In 1530, having secured his coronation by the pope as emperor in Bologna, he returned to the

Empire with the aim of finding a theological formula which would bridge the differences between the faiths. When this failed, he pushed successive popes to undertake a reform of the Church, by which he hoped both to reinvigorate Catholicism and to remedy the sort of abuses of which Protestants complained. Charles believed a General Council of the Church the best vehicle for undertaking this reform, but the popes were wary lest a council usurp their prerogatives. It was only in 1545 that the General Council assembled at Trent and it promptly affirmed Catholic doctrines which were inimical to most Protestants.

In anticipation of a military showdown in the Empire, Charles prepared in 1545 detailed 'painted maps' of the German lands, showing 'the location of towns as well as the distances between them, and rivers and mountains'. Charles also prepared the political ground. Instead of launching a religious war, he moved against the leading Protestant princes with the excuse that they had occupied territories to which they were not entitled. This divided the enemy and so prepared the way for Charles's stunning victory at Mühlberg in 1547. His victory was, however, too complete to last. Five years later, a Protestant league for 'liberty and freedom', but supported by the French king, put Charles to flight.

Charles handed over to Ferdinand the negotiation of a peace in the Empire, which following discussions at Augsburg in 1555 gave its princes and lords the right to choose between Catholicism and Lutheranism. By this time, the emperor had reached the end of his physical and mental strength. Alternating between vacancy and weeping, he spent his final years as emperor taking clocks apart and having his servants make them tick in unison. After 1555, he abdicated his realms and retired to live in the monastery of Yuste in Castile. He died there in 1558. The politics of concession had found their limit in the struggle over religion.

Chapter 3
'As if the king of each': 16th and 17th centuries

Kingdoms and coronations

The lands over which Charles held sway were not only compared at the time to the Roman Empire but also deemed more magnificent, exceeding its land mass many times over. Charles toyed with this conceit, both in his emblem of the Pillars of Hercules and in organizing 'triumphs' in the Roman fashion to celebrate his victories. The extent of Charles's lands and kingdoms seemed to fulfil the Renaissance dream of a 'world empire' in which Christians would live in harmony under a single ruler, who would usher in a renewed Golden Age. A complementary reading, based on apocalyptic prophecies, saw Charles as 'the last emperor', whose reign presaged the final showdown with Antichrist and the Day of Judgement. These predictions comported with the mystique of dynastic mission promoted by Charles's predecessors.

Charles, however, did not understand 'world monarchy' in political and institutional terms. He did not try to unite his disparate realms but ruled instead through the separate governments of his individual lands and kingdoms. Although convinced that his realms should remain in some sort of association after his death, he did not press for them to have a single successor, for he knew that neither his son, Philip, nor his brother, Ferdinand, would willingly concede power to the other. Instead, he apportioned his

Spanish possessions together with the Low Countries to Philip, while the Austrian lands remained with Ferdinand, the better to support his Hungarian and Bohemian kingdoms. Ferdinand, who had been elected king of the Romans in 1531, also succeeded to the imperial title following his brother's abdication.

Charles governed his possessions not as a universal ruler but instead, as a later Spanish jurist explained, 'as if the king who keeps them together were only the king of each'. His many lands were thus run as a 'composite monarchy', with its parts united only by the identity of the sovereign. For Charles, the reason for this was straightforward. He wrote to his son, Philip, later Philip II of Spain, that 'each nation must be approached with respect and dealt with differently according to the nature of its peoples'. Charles thus worked in concert with traditional institutions and adhered to the separate customs of his different realms. Local nobilities, provincial freedoms, urban councils, the rights of diets and parliaments to be consulted, and antique laws thus remained for the most part in place, undisturbed. As Philip II of Spain was to learn, to challenge any of these could provoke a political crisis.

Deference to established rights and liberties was not only the consequence of political expediency. It was also written into the most important legislative acts to which Charles and his successors committed themselves. During their separate coronations and investitures, as kings of Castile, Aragon, Bohemia, and Hungary, and as Holy Roman Emperors, successive Habsburg rulers swore to maintain the freedoms and liberties of their subjects. In Castile and Aragon, where there was no formal crowning but only a public proclamation, the heir to the throne nonetheless promised before the Cortes and Corts General to uphold the rights of his subjects in return for their loyalty. In the Aragonese Corts General, the assembled representatives swore an oath to the ruler that effectively bound both sides in a mutual contract: 'We, who are as good as you, swear to you, who are no better than us, to accept you as our king and sovereign, provided you observe all our liberties and laws, but if not, not.' In the counties and duchies of the Low Countries, the ruler swore on his first visit to each to abide by the laws and freedoms of the land. The texts of these 'Joyous Entries' were often printed and distributed as proof of the new sovereign's commitments.

In the Holy Roman Empire and Hungary, coronation oaths were expanded by formal agreements or 'capitulations' decided by the diets. In the Empire, these capitulations were published for the first time in 1519. In Hungary, Ferdinand and his successors even agreed at the time of their coronation to permit the nobility to take up arms against them should they violate its privileges. Ferdinand later failed in his attempt to have the disagreeable 'right of resistance' written out of Hungary's laws. In Portugal, which fell to Philip II in 1580 following a succession crisis, the oath of the ruler was similarly supplemented by a long list of conditions. Philip solemnly swore to maintain these at a special session of the Portuguese Cortes.

In Bohemia, an unusual arrangement prevailed. During the 15th century, Bohemia had been swept by the Hussite heresy, which was a forerunner of the Reformation. Religious peace in the kingdom was only secured in the 1430s when the Emperor Sigismund, who was also king of Bohemia, agreed to the Compacts of Prague. These recognized the separate practices of the Bohemian Church, particularly in regard to the celebration of the Mass and the organization of the clergy. The Compacts were subsequently denounced by the pope as heretical. Nevertheless, at their coronations the Bohemian kings, including Ferdinand and his son, Maximilian II, agreed to maintain the Compacts, even though they were upholding provisions that were supposedly heretical.

Governments and courts

The preferred method of 16th-century Habsburg rule was 'conciliar'. This meant that Habsburg monarchs practised, where they could, government by committee, and functions were devolved to meetings made up largely of experts. The heads of these committees, the secretaries or 'super-clerks', often reported directly to the ruler, thus preparing the way for what would later become cabinet government.

Even in Castile, where conciliar government was most developed, grandees nevertheless dominated the Council of State, which took the most important decisions involving foreign affairs and the broad outlines of policy. Leading aristocrats occupied a similar position in the Council of State in the Habsburg Low Countries. They also filled the offices of governors and viceroys abroad, although in the Low Countries female relatives of the sovereign were often preferred. More and more, however, the real work of government was taken over by councils staffed by administrators. In Castile, the Council of Finance increasingly determined policy, and in the Low Countries the Privy Council, which advised the ruler or his regent on domestic affairs, became influential at the expense of the Council of State.

The administration of justice also became more professional. Superior courts that had once been headed up by aristocratic placemen and noble assessors gave way to courts that were run by trained lawyers. The lawyers had often been educated in Roman Law, which put a premium on the statutory law, as opposed to the vague and often unwritten customary law. By demanding written proofs, Roman Law disadvantaged many noblemen and others, whose rights had never been formally recorded. The Romanist tag, 'What pleases the prince has the force of the law', also empowered monarchs to legislate by decree, interfere in the business of the courts, and override established rights. As the president of the highest court in the Low Countries observed, 'Presumption is always in favour of the justice of the prince himself, to such an extent that if the prince command something contrary to divine law, such as the hanging or murder of someone whose trial is still under way, or similar things, he must be obeyed.'

In large areas over which the Habsburgs ruled, however, conciliar government was barely possible, for the foundations for the effective exercise of the ruler's power were missing. In the Austrian lands, the ducal administration was synonymous only with the management of the private resources of the ruler. Diets and their committees exercised many of the attributes of government in the Austrian lands, also having a say in the choice of the chief minister. In Bohemia and Hungary, the parliaments similarly controlled the government, to the extent that in Bohemia almost all the principal officers of the crown were appointees of the diet.

In his 'Court Ordinance' of 1527, Ferdinand established in Vienna a group of councils to assist him in the business of rule—a Court Chancellery, Court Treasury, and Privy Council. To their number, he added in 1556 a Court War Council. Historians have conventionally seen the ordinance as 'centralizing' and 'modernizing', and as an attempt to weld together Ferdinand's Austrian, Hungarian, and Bohemian possessions into a single administrative unit. This was neither Ferdinand's aim nor his legacy. The various councils had shifting competences, but at no time did they provide administrative unity and the type of centralized government for which historians look.

Ferdinand established separate councils of regency in Bohemia and Hungary, which became increasingly effective vehicles of government and justice. Their very success, however, underlined the disunity of the Habsburg lands in Central Europe. In the final years of his reign, Ferdinand partitioned his possessions, in accordance with the Habsburg tradition of dividing up the dynasty's possessions among sons. Ferdinand's eldest son, Maximilian, who had been elected king of the Romans in 1562, followed Ferdinand as emperor two years later. He also succeeded him as king in Bohemia and Hungary, and as duke of Upper and Lower Austria. Ferdinand entrusted his other sons, Ferdinand and Charles, with respectively the Tyrol and the duchies of Styria,

Carinthia, and Carniola, which were also lifted out of the institutional framework established in 1527. Ferdinand thus bequeathed to his sons a divided inheritance.

The idea that Habsburg rule stood for something more than just lands and kingdoms connected through the person of the ruler was manifested in courts and ceremony. The royal and imperial courts in or near Madrid, and in Vienna and in Prague were places of monarchical display, intended for visual, intellectual, and emotional effect. Courtly life was built on strict etiquette and elaborate spectacle, in which the monarch himself became, in the words of a shrewd Spanish observer, 'but a ceremony'. This aspect was combined in Vienna and Prague with the exotic and the latest scientific accomplishments, including an observatory and a zoo, with monkeys, a lion, and an ostrich (the elephant died too early to be accommodated). Close beside the Hofburg palace in Vienna, Maximilian II also constructed in the 1560s an arena for tournaments and ceremonial displays of horsemanship that followed the techniques of classical Greece. Equipped with horses from Andalusia in Spain, which were subsequently cross-bred at Lipizza (today Lipica, in Slovenia) near Trieste, Maximilian's foundation provided the basis of what would later become Vienna's Spanish Riding School. For his part, Maximilian II's brother, Ferdinand of the Tyrol, had at Castle Ambras outside Innsbruck his own extensive (and surviving) collection of 'wonders'—pieces of Samurai armour, unusual lumps of coral, and disturbing portraits.

The courts of Central Europe were dwarfed by Philip II's Escorial palace outside Madrid, which was described in the 1580s by some visiting Japanese noblemen as 'a thing more magnificent than any we have seen till now or imagined seeing'. Less a palace than a mausoleum, the Escorial had as its heart a monastery and the king's collection of 7,000 relics, including ten whole bodies of saints and martyrs, 144 heads, and 306 miscellaneous arms and legs. The courts of Spain's representatives abroad were equally splendid. At a time when monarchs were increasingly hidden by ceremony, the Spanish viceroys in the New World advertised their public presence in spectacular processions. With their grand staircases, broad balconies, and grand squares, the royal palaces in Mexico City and Lima were designed to show off the person of the viceroy as the substitute for an absent king's majesty.

The Habsburg courts were magnets for petitioners, for artists seeking commissions, and for scholars, wizards, and alchemists looking for patronage. They were also places where leading aristocrats, prelates, and adventurers from across the Habsburgs lands met, negotiated with one another and the ruler, and arranged marriages. Many even bought property close by. Habsburg princes and wives passing to and from Spain and Central Europe were often accompanied by extensive retinues, which needed to be physically accommodated. The Habsburg courts thus functioned not only as cosmopolitan microcosms of the far-flung Habsburg possessions but also as meeting places, where Czechs, Hungarians, Flemings, Germans, and Spaniards came together in the ruler's presence and in his service.

Religion and resistance

Charles V's son, Philip II of Spain was uncompromising in matters of the Catholic faith. As he explained several times, 'Rather than suffer the least injury to religion and the service of God, I would lose all my states and a hundred lives if I had them, for I do not intend to rule over heretics.' Historians have recently drawn attention to Philip's love of dancing, tournaments, and womanizing, but the 'Black Legend' that surrounds his reign is not easily dispelled. Philip persecuted all whose allegiance to Catholicism might be suspected, with the consequence that humanist enquiry was blunted in Spain and a scholarly 'self-censorship' took root. Students were forbidden to travel abroad for study, lest they encounter unwelcome beliefs. Nascent Protestant communities in Valladolid and Seville were rooted out, with about a hundred people burnt. Philip enthusiastically recommended the expulsion of the Spanish Muslims, who were a legacy of the time when most of Spain had been under Islamic rule. Some Muslims were Ottoman 'fifth columnists', but Spanish Jews were not, and they too were hounded from Philip's possessions.

Philip's private apartments in the Escorial overlooked gardens and, beyond these, a bare landscape, parched for most of the year against a cloudless sky. The starkness of aspect had its counterpart in the uncompromising manner in which Philip conducted policy. When in the 1560s the aristocrats in the Low Countries resisted his administrative reforms, he excluded them from government. When they made common cause with the small but vociferous minority of Protestants and demanded toleration, he refused concessions. When disaffection spilled over into rebellion, he sent in an army and imposed a regime that executed almost two thousand heretics and rebels. The Archduke Charles of Styria, who was no friend of Protestants, urged Philip to win over his subjects by 'kindness and compassion', but Philip preferred the type of rule where, in the words of his leading general, 'every individual has the feeling that one fine night or morning the house will fall in on him'.

The Cortes in Castile resisted sending money abroad, and so Philip raised the money for his army in the Low Countries by taxing its cities. This expedient proved insufficient and his unpaid troops mutinied, ravaging the land and, in 1576, sacking Antwerp. Although by negotiating a deal with the aristocratic leaders in the southern provinces of the Low Countries, Philip was able to hold onto a part of his possessions, the rest was permanently lost to Spain, largely on account of his intransigence. The seven northern provinces formed after 1581 an independent Protestant republic, the United Provinces of the Netherlands. Even so, Philip not only maintained the war in the Low Countries, but also coupled it to a planned invasion of England. His Grand Armada perished in 1588. Over a long period, he discussed in all seriousness a plan to use the Philippines as the springboard for the invasion and conversion of China.

Ferdinand was readier to make concessions and it was he who agreed in 1555 to the Peace of Augsburg, which permitted princes and rulers in the Empire to embrace Lutheranism. His court was open to 'tender consciences' and he personally pressed the pope to make compromises that would open the way to a religious accommodation. His son, Maximilian II, was even more tolerant. In private he averred that he was neither Catholic nor Protestant, but simply a Christian. Even so, he kept Luther's Bible at his bedside and welcomed Protestant nobles and preachers to his court. He also cancelled his father's anti-Jewish legislation and championed in particular the rights of Jews in Prague. Their numbers increased in the city from a few dozen to several thousand, making it the largest centre of Jewish population in Europe after Constantinople.

By the middle decades of the 16th century, Protestantism had made extensive inroads into the Austrian lands, to the extent that most monasteries were abandoned and few churches had Catholic priests. Even in the surviving Tyrolean abbey of Stams, nearly all the monks' cells were found to contain Lutheran pamphlets. Whatever his religious persuasion, it made political sense for Maximilian II to give way to the demand of the mainly Protestant diets that he grant confessional freedom in the Austrian lands. To do otherwise might jeopardize the taxes the diets voted.

Much the same situation prevailed elsewhere in Maximilian's lands. In Hungary, Lutheranism had taken a foothold in the kingdom's cities as early as the 1520s. But it was the sterner Protestantism of John Calvin that won the countryside. Calvinism's stress on divine providence suited Hungarians as it provided an explanation for their country's occupation by the Turks and Habsburgs. With its call for a Godly Reformation of morals and conduct, Calvinism also showed how God's grace might be enlisted in the struggle against the foreigner. In Bohemia, Lutheranism also prospered, side by side with the more moderate branch of Hussitism, known as Utraquism. Other Protestant sects found special refuge in the eastern Bohemian crown land of Moravia, which was considered at the time 'a melting pot for all possible heresies on earth'. One commentator listed twenty-five separate heresies there—Adamites, for whom godliness meant nakedness; Demoniacs, whose faith caused them to rage like madmen; Concubites, who refused marriage, and so on.

Neither of Maximilian's brothers, Ferdinand of the Tyrol and Charles of Styria, shared the emperor's religious ambiguity but remained steadfastly in the Catholic camp. In 1579, they jointly embraced a scheme for the re-Catholicization of the Austrian lands. Persecution and the forced closure of Protestant churches were to be combined with the revival of the monasteries and a new stress on education in the Catholic faith. It is usual to attribute the gains that followed to the Jesuit teaching order, but that is to follow the propaganda both of the Jesuits and of their enemies. More was owed to reforming bishops who laboured to rebuild Catholic schools and monasteries. In the 1590s, the bishops of Passau and Vienna took the lead in suppressing a peasant uprising in Upper and Lower Austria, after which they released their troops on the countryside to compel conversion.

Emperor Rudolf II, who succeeded his father Maximilian in 1576, was never less than fickle. A recluse and prodigious patron of the arts, he was too easily drawn to the intellectually exotic. As his brothers reported, 'His Majesty is interested only in wizards, alchemists, Kabbalists and the like, sparing no expense to find all kinds of treasures, learn secrets and use scandalous ways of harming his enemies... He also has a whole library of magic books. He strives all the time to eliminate God completely so that he may in future serve a different master.' Nevertheless, from around 1600, when the so-called 'Spanish faction' gained ascendancy in his court at Prague, Rudolf began to press the cause of the Catholic or Counter-Reformation. In Hungary, he arrested the leading Protestant noblemen on trumped up charges and then, in 1604, banned Protestantism altogether, sending in troops to close down churches.

The Transylvanian principality was the creation of the Hungarian king, John Szapolyai, elected in 1526 as a rival to Ferdinand. Unable to make good his claim to the whole of the kingdom, Szapolyai had retreated to the highlands of Transylvania, which was internationally recognized in 1570 as an independent principality under its own prince, who was elected by the Transylvanian diet. The Transylvanian nobility, who were mostly Calvinist, supported their co-religionists in Hungary against Rudolf II. Defeated on the battlefield, Rudolf was forced to back down, agreeing in 1606, in the Treaty of Vienna, to full religious freedom in Hungary. Sensing his weakness, the Bohemian diet obliged Rudolf to make similar concessions, including the right to hold Protestant services on crown and church lands. In the Letter of Majesty of 1609, Rudolf agreed that a permanent sub-committee of the diet, known as the Defenders, should police the religious settlement. He promised that, 'Henceforth no free noblemen or inhabitants of town and villages, including peasants, should be forced by a higher authority or indeed anyone, be they churchmen or lay men, to give up their religion or be compelled to change religion in any way whatsoever.' Rudolf gave similar rights to the townsfolk and nobilities of Upper and Lower Austria.

The military frontier

For three decades after 1526, there was almost continuous war between the Habsburgs and the Ottomans in Central Europe. Not only was Vienna put under siege in 1529, but Ottoman skirmishers also fought and raided deep in Austrian territory.

In 1541 Suleiman occupied the central portion of Hungary. The Church of Our Lady ('Matthias Church') in Buda, which is now Hungary's premier tourist attraction, was converted into a mosque. Almost every year Suleiman launched campaigns westward from occupied Hungary and attempted to prise yet more territory from Ferdinand I.

Suleiman died on campaign in 1566. Thereafter, the conflict abated, its principal theatre moving to the Mediterranean. Raiding by garrison troops and probing expeditions nevertheless continued. Maximilian II's expert on the Ottoman Empire wrote, 'Like a raging dog, the Turk is always roaring around our borders trying to break in, now in this place, now in that.' Most raids were aimed at cattle rustling and capturing prisoners for the burgeoning trade in ransoms, but they could spill over into full warfare. Plundering expeditions and skirmishes organized by the Turkish pasha of Bosnia formed the prelude to the 'Long War' of 1593–1606.

From the mid-16th century onwards, military campaigning frequently bogged down in long sieges leading to military stalemates. The reason was the development of strongly fortified positions, often including whole towns, which were designed by Italian and Spanish engineers according to the latest military innovations. Surrounded by bastions and thick, earth-backed walls, the new fortresses were difficult to capture and the garrison often had to be starved into surrender. Large and expensive armies were needed to conduct a successful siege and to cut off the defenders' supply routes.

The kingdom of Croatia, which was joined to the kingdom of Hungary, occupied a strategically vital position, commanding the roadways that led from Ottoman territory to the Austrian duchies of Carinthia, Carniola, and Styria. Ferdinand I began in the 1520s the policy of settling refugees, who were mostly Serbs, on Croatian territory, giving them land in exchange for military service.

The frontiersmen numbered about 6,000 men in the 1570s, but their discipline was poor. As one Carniolan nobleman reported, 'They love to rob, steal and plunder and could not exist without brigandage and murder.' Some frontiersmen also took to the sea as pirates, preying indiscriminately on shipping in the Adriatic. Nevertheless, the frontier troops constituted the 'outer bastion' of the Habsburg defensive system. Their loyalty was such that in the 17th century they were even deployed on behalf of the crown against Hungarian rebels.

The costs of warfare were high. In the 1570s, years of relative peace, the upkeep and repair of fortresses and garrisons in Hungary cost 1.6 million florins, and the Croatian military frontier a further 600,000 florins. The financing of the Croatian frontier was borne directly by the diets of the neighbouring Austrian duchies. The other Austrian provinces gave a further 600,000 florins to the overall budget. Since the imperial diet contributed only intermittently, this left an annual deficit of one million florins. It used to be thought that the shortfall was covered by remittances from Spain, but Philip II needed all the funds he had to prosecute the war in the Low Countries. What we now know is that deft financial management in Hungary yielded a substantial income. Resources were harnessed, particularly in respect of toll rights and other monopolies, and royal lands that had been given away were repossessed. By the 1570s, the Hungarian treasury had an annual income of up to 650,000 florins; other funds were taken at source for military purposes and never went through the treasury's books. The rest was borrowed, seldom to be repaid.

In 1606 a lasting peace was made with the Ottoman sultan. By this time, the weakness of Turkish arms was clear. Too much was lost to corruption, while Ottoman tactics and logistics had not kept up with military innovation. Until this point, the Ottoman threat had blunted the struggle against Protestantism, for the Turks could exploit any religious conflict in the

Habsburg lands. To fight the Ottomans, the Habsburg armies also needed the taxes voted by the Protestant diets in the Austrian lands. Protestantism had made huge gains during the reign of Rudolf II, acquiring legal recognition throughout most of Central Europe. But with peace on the border, the day of religious reckoning was not far off.

Chapter 4
In the service of the faith: 17th and 18th centuries

Ferdinand II

Ferdinand of Styria, the future Ferdinand II, not only rebuilt Habsburg power in Central Europe but also changed decisively the religious and political complexion of the region. He restored Catholicism to a large part of his dominions and broke the power of the diets and nobility in the Austrian and Bohemian lands. Ferdinand took enormous risks, but historians rightly regard his reign as a turning point in Habsburg history.

Ferdinand was the first Habsburg to attend university, in Jesuit Ingolstadt. His mother's verdict on Ferdinand's education in Catholic doctrine was telling—'nothing sown in this fertile soil seems to perish'. Shortly after completing his studies in 1595, Ferdinand took over from his father, Charles, the government of Styria, Carinthia, and Carniola, but soon departed on pilgrimage to Rome. On the way there, he stopped at the Loreto, the house of Jesus's childhood, miraculously transported from Nazareth to Italy in the 13th century. There, according to later reports, he swore a solemn oath to remove all Protestants from his possessions.

The story of Ferdinand's oath may be no truer than the legend of the holy house. Even so, upon his return home Ferdinand redoubled the persecution of Protestants in Styria, Carinthia, and Carniola that had been begun by his father. At the time of his inauguration as ruler of these provinces, Ferdinand had sworn to maintain the 'rights, liberties and praiseworthy customs' of his subjects. Now, he found that these conflicted with his conscience and, relying upon the conceits of Roman Law, he repudiated his previous promises, asserting that it was his right as ruler to act without legal constraint. Protestant churches were closed, books burnt, and attendance at mass enforced by troops. Between 1598 and 1606, 11,000 Protestants emigrated.

During the last years of his reign, the Emperor Rudolf II was harried by his brother, Matthias, who sought to replace him, eventually becoming emperor in 1612. Matthias has not done well by historians, for whom he is vacillating, duplicitous, and incompetent. Over the preceding decades, Matthias had indeed been all things to all men, but once in power as emperor and king of Bohemia and Hungary, he swung round to support the Counter-Reformation. In Bohemia, he undermined the Letter of Majesty, ceded by Rudolf in 1609, exploiting the gaps and ambiguities in its provisions. He censored publications and, where he could, excluded non-Catholics from office. Recognizing that he did not have long to live and not having children of his own, Matthias championed his cousin, Ferdinand, as his future heir and adopted son. To guarantee the succession, Matthias sought to have Ferdinand elected king in Bohemia and Hungary even in his own lifetime.

Matthias trod warily. In what has been called 'a triumph of management and manipulation', he outmanoeuvred the Protestant caucus in the Bohemian diet. Matthias achieved Ferdinand's election as king by having him promise to maintain the traditional rights of the country, including by implication the Letter of Majesty, and not to interfere in Bohemian affairs in Matthias's own lifetime. In Hungary, Matthias published conjointly with Ferdinand a coronation diploma that recognized the provisions of the Treaty of Vienna, affirming that 'the exercise of religion shall everywhere be free'. In all his future dealings with the Hungarians, Ferdinand kept by this commitment, notwithstanding the pain to his conscience and the affront to his authority. Quite possibly, he would have kept his promise to the Bohemians too had not events dictated otherwise.

In 1618, the Protestant Defenders, appointed under the terms of the Letter of Majesty to protect religious freedom, overthrew the government in Bohemia. In the 'Defenestration of Prague', they ejected three of Matthias's officials from the window of the royal castle. The men landed, almost unscathed, in a dung heap—later accounts reported the intervention of angels. The Defenders' complaint was that Matthias had ordered the destruction of two Protestant churches built, controversially, on crown land. The coup launched by the Defenders was supported by only a minority of Bohemian noblemen, but these now dizzily declared Ferdinand's previous election void. In Ferdinand's place, they elected a political madman, Frederick of the Palatinate, whose wizards and Calvinist clergy had convinced him that he was destined to fulfil a divine purpose, hitherto hidden in alchemical mysteries. Meanwhile, Ferdinand succeeded as emperor, on Matthias's death in 1619.

Notwithstanding his election as emperor, Ferdinand's position rapidly unravelled. Moravia, Hungary, and Transylvania joined Bohemia in a military alliance. The diets of Upper and Lower Austria also supported the rebels. Ferdinand did not bow down, however, for he had a full hand of aces. Over the preceding years, he had established close relations with neighbouring Bavaria and Saxony, and with his Spanish relatives. The cost of their support was great in terms of commitments given, marriages made, and territories promised. Ferdinand's concessions ensured nonetheless that, upon hearing of the events in Prague, Philip III of Spain's immediate response should be to order an armada to set sail for Bohemia. (Like Shakespeare, Philip imagined Bohemia to have a coastline.) While a Spanish army from the Low Countries invaded the Palatinate, a largely Bavarian one destroyed the Bohemian army in less than two hours outside Prague. The Hungarians hurried to make peace, on generous terms, with Ferdinand—he stuck by his earlier commitment to maintain religious freedom in Hungary and even agreed to appoint a Protestant first minister. All resistance in the Austrian lands crumbled, opening the way to a largely successful renewal of the work of conversion.

Destroyed militarily, Bohemia was now crushed politically. Ferdinand's approach to the prostrate kingdom rested on two doubtful propositions. The first was that the Bohemians had rebelled 'collectively', which meant that the entire nation might be punished. The second was that all rights were of the ruler's gift and that he was therefore empowered to rescind them. In the 'Renewed Constitution' of 1627, these ideas coalesced to yield an ordinance of extreme severity. Ferdinand declared the Bohemian succession no longer elective, but hereditary in the house of Habsburg. He removed the legislative capacity of the diet, declaring instead the priority of royal decrees and that the diet's main role was to graciously concede the taxes asked of it. He prohibited outright all Protestant worship. The only option available to non-Catholics was emigration—between a third and a half of the Bohemian nobility went into exile. The Letter of Majesty guaranteeing religious freedom was, literally, slashed down the middle (Figure 4).

The Thirty Years War

The war in Bohemia was the first phase in a series of contests that are known collectively as the 'Thirty Years War' (1618–48). Each phase, however, bore within it seeds of future conflict, to such an extent that contemporaries considered the fighting to constitute a single prolonged period of warfare. The Thirty Years War drew in most of Europe's principal powers—the Netherlands, Spain, Sweden, France, and the leading German principalities. For some, the motivation was religious; for others, opportunistic. Side by

4. The Letter of Majesty, 1609, in which Rudolf II gave religious freedom to Bohemia. The charter has been slashed to invalidate its contents.

side with the main theatre of conflict in the Holy Roman Empire were 'side-shows' that were often equally bloody—in the Low Countries where war between Spain and the Protestant northern provinces was renewed; in the Pyrenees where the Spanish fought the French; and further afield in Muscovy where a proxy war over Smolensk broke out between Russians and Poles, urged on by the Swedes.

The first decade went well for Ferdinand II. Having vanquished the Bohemians and Frederick of the Palatinate, he successfully took on their Protestant allies. Confident in his victory, Ferdinand ordered in 1629 that all church properties in the Holy Roman Empire seized by Protestant princes over the previous decades be restored. The 'Edict of Restitution' unleashed a further round of conflict, with the Swedes intervening from the north to support their co-religionists. In the Peace of Prague of 1635, Ferdinand made peace with the German princes, effectively withdrawing the Edict. French forces now took the lead in maintaining the fight against Ferdinand, in alliance with the Swedes. The war thus largely lost its religious character becoming instead a political contest between France and the Habsburgs. In this phase of the struggle, the French supported the revolt of Catalonia against Philip IV of Spain and the secession of Portugal from the Spanish crown in 1640. The last year of the war saw a Swedish army occupy Prague Castle—the site of the Defenestration that had begun the conflict three decades before.

The Thirty Years War claimed eight million lives—and this is without counting deaths in the 'peripheral' military actions to which it gave rise. The Peace of Westphalia, which ended the conflict, was mostly concerned with nuts and bolts—where borders should be changed, rights to territory affirmed, and the title of elector conveyed. It affirmed, however, that the princes of the Holy Roman Empire might choose their own religion, but it allowed their subjects the right to practise their own beliefs too (within certain limits). In future, disputes over church property and the extent of freedom of conscience were to be a matter for the courts to decide—and the central courts of the Empire were renewed specifically to this end, with equal numbers of Protestant and Catholic judges appointed. The type of militarized Catholicism that Ferdinand II had sought to impose was no longer possible. An important exemption, however, applied to the Habsburg lands, meaning that its ruler, after 1637 Ferdinand III, was not obliged to permit freedom of worship. The labour of reconversion undertaken in Bohemia and the Austrian lands was not, therefore, to be reversed.

The text of the Peace of Westphalia was a bestseller that went through thirty editions in just the first year of its promulgation. Interpretations of its content differed, even at the time. One author (Johann Jacob Moser) composed no less than seventy volumes attempting to explain the character of the Holy Roman Empire as shaped by the Peace. It was considered by some rulers to give scope for complete political dominion and even 'sovereignty' over their lands (although this word was deliberately left out of the final draft of the Peace). Others saw in its text a confederal arrangement, which preserved the power of central institutions. In fact, as one commentator observed, the Peace of Westphalia had created a unique structure that did not fit into any established category of state, on which account he called it 'an irregular body, akin to a monstrosity'.

Historians have generally considered the Thirty Years War to be a conflict that Germany and the Habsburgs both lost. The Holy Roman Empire's fragmentation into small states was not reversed, while the strengthening of the powers belonging to local rulers made the coordination of policy under the emperor even harder to obtain. Nevertheless, the Habsburgs still possessed considerable influence and resources within the Empire. Their territorial losses had been small, being mainly confined to the peripheral provinces of Upper and Lower Lusatia (ceded to Saxony in 1635). The emperor was, moreover, the natural ally of those minor rulers who felt under threat from the local hegemonies practised by the larger principalities, and he was still viewed as the embodiment of German unity, standing above the Empire's political divisions and giving leadership to its jostling princes.

Ferdinand III and, subsequently, Leopold I did not act as if the Peace of Westphalia had diminished their influence. Ferdinand personally presided for eighteen months over the diet that met in Regensburg from 1652 to 1654, pushing for the reinvigoration of central institutions of justice and, in vain, for the formation of a standing army. His son, Leopold, led the struggle against Louis XIV's encroachments into the territory of the Empire, joining the Dutch in 1672 to defend the Rhine frontier and, in 1688, founding the League of Augsburg to protect the Palatinate. All in all,

Leopold was at war with Louis XIV for almost twenty years. The Holy Roman Empire was still Habsburg, indissolubly linked to the identity of the ruler.

Hungary and the 'work of instauration'

Leopold I's advisers were divided over policy, with some advocating a western orientation against the French and others pressing for expansion eastwards, against the Ottomans. In fact, the two theatres were linked. Louis XIV gave financial support to rebellions against Habsburg rule launched from Transylvania, which was a Turkish vassal state, and he took advantage of the Habsburg armies being occupied in the east to renew pressure in the west. At critical moments, Leopold had to abandon campaigns against the Ottomans, redeploying his resources from the Danube to the Rhine. In 1664, therefore, Leopold was unable to consolidate a victory against the Turks, fought at St Gotthard in western Hungary, for fear that Louis XIV would invade Spain. Instead Leopold concluded with the sultan the Treaty of Vasvár, which restored the territorial status quo.

Disappointed at the poor terms of the Treaty of Vasvár, some of the leading Hungarian magnates plotted to depose Leopold, counting not only on French but bizarrely also on Ottoman support for their plans. The conspiracy was prolonged in its making and its architects were incapable of secrecy. After giving them several warnings, Leopold arrested the leaders, occupied their castles, and sent them to the block. A heavy-handed investigation yielded a further 2,000 suspects, several hundred of whom were proceeded against by special courts.

In the wake of the conspiracy's suppression, Leopold's advisers pushed him to use the opportunity to bring Hungary into line and, as one pamphleteer recommended, 'squeeze the Hungarians into Bohemian breeches'. Leopold was certainly tough, but at no time did he subject Hungary to the type of regime that his grandfather,

Ferdinand II, had imposed on Bohemia. Notoriously, however, he clamped down on Calvinist preaching in Hungary and, when the Calvinist clergy ignored his prohibition, he instructed the arrest in 1674 of several hundred preachers. Of these, forty were condemned to be galley slaves. Given every opportunity to escape, the preachers nonetheless walked resolutely to their fate in Naples. Shortly after embarkation, they were dramatically rescued from the galleys by a Dutch flotilla.

The theatricality of the preachers' suffering and escape did much to undermine Leopold's reputation in Protestant Europe. Persecution was, however, not only internationally damaging but also increasingly pointless. By this time, the energy of the Catholic clergy was making dramatic inroads in Hungary, to the extent that most of the aristocracy had forsaken Protestantism. The gilded magnificence of the restored Catholic churches, many of which were now rebuilt in the style of the baroque, and education through plays, processions, and preaching in the vernacular, did much to win over the countryside. Tellingly, the most prominent of the galley slaves, Ferenc Fóris Otrokócsi, subsequently converted to Catholicism, forsaking his refuge in Oxford for a professorship at the Catholic university of Trnava in Hungary.

In the 1680s, the Ottoman Empire renewed its westward advance. Leopold responded by working together with the pope to construct a 'holy alliance' that brought to his aid Poland, Bavaria, and Protestant Saxony, as well as a huge slice of church wealth—one-third of ecclesiastical property in the Austrian lands was sold off to fund the allies. In 1683, Leopold's commanders and allies smashed an Ottoman army besieging Vienna. Three years later, Leopold captured Buda and liberated most of Hungary. Habsburg armies pushed south into the Balkans, briefly occupying Skopje, which is now the capital of Macedonia and only 200 kilometres north of the Aegean coast. Once again, however, warfare in the west obliged Leopold to withdraw his troops and abandon his Balkan conquests. After a short flurry of resistance, however, Transylvania capitulated to Leopold in return for guarantees of religious freedom.

Following the reconquest of Hungary, the issue arose of what to do with the country. Leopold acted swiftly, obliging a cowed Hungarian diet to recognize the Habsburgs as hereditary and not elected kings. All else, he left to committees to decide. Of these, the real work was done by a sub-commission headed by Cardinal Kollonich, which met on some eighty occasions in 1688. The 'Work of Instauration' was the fruit of its labours—a blueprint for the complete reform of Hungary, running to several hundred pages of dense text. The kingdom was to be given new laws and institutions, the peasants to be relieved of most of their burdens, the rights of the nobility to be trimmed, and an infrastructure of roads, hospitals, and schools to be established. In the territories recently reconquered from the Ottomans, only those nobles who could prove their titles were to be restored to their family's former properties. The rest was to be assigned to the Hungarian treasury and used to support a programme of 'impopulation'. Kollonich's sub-commission recommended that care be taken to bring in German settlers, 'so that the kingdom or at least a good part of it be gradually Germanized, and that the Hungarian blood which is inclined to rebellion and restlessness be diluted with the German, thus being brought to love and obey its natural hereditary king and lord'.

Leopold knew that to impose the 'Work of Instauration' would prompt civil war and he ignored most of the sub-commission's recommendations. Nevertheless, he took up its proposals for impopulation. In 1689 Leopold issued a decree offering advantageous terms to German settlers who came to the newly conquered parts of Hungary. As it turned out, over the next two years, the largest influx into the kingdom was by Serbs who had supported the Habsburg march to Skopje and now feared Ottoman reprisals. The settlement of several tens of thousands of Serb families in southern Hungary decisively altered the region's demographic balance and eventually contributed to this part of Hungary being given to Yugoslavia in 1920.

Under Leopold's successor, Charles VI, a further expansion took place at the expense of the Ottoman Empire, with the acquisition in 1718 of the Banat of Timişoara. In just five years, 20,000 Germans moved to the Banat, which was otherwise mainly populated by Romanians and Serbs. They were joined by Armenians and Italians, recruited respectively as leather-workers and silkworm cultivators. Such was the demand for labour that little attention was paid to religious affiliation. Recruitment of foreign settlers bore many of the hallmarks of colonization to the New World—with glossy brochures promising a paradise, offers of free passage, and new towns planned on a grid pattern. The Banat, which occupies a space one and a half times the size of Wales and is now split between Romania and Serbia, remains to this day one of Europe's most ethnically diverse regions.

The global Habsburgs

In the 16th and 17th centuries, the Habsburg dominions encompassed the world. The pretensions of Frederick III and Maximilian I—the acrostics, fantastic wallpaper, and ambitious genealogies—had been geographically realized. The reach of the Habsburg family, divided into its two branches, stretched from what is now Ukraine to the Americas and beyond, to the Philippines and the coast of China.

In much of the Habsburg New World, however, power was exercised unevenly. In the viceroyalty of Peru, Spanish rule barely extended beyond the highlands. Much of the coastal strip and the lowlands belonged to the indigenous people, whose resistance was stiffened by renegade Spanish settlers and disaffected soldiers. In the Amazon basin, Jesuits and friars carved out territories using their own private armies, and corralled the natives into 'concentrated villages', the better to aid their control and conversion. Except for Manila, Spanish rule in the Philippines was never more than a chimera. Even in Mexico, where colonial government was more thoroughly entrenched, settlers established vast semi-independent lordships. The 130,000 square kilometres belonging in the later 16th century to Martin Cortés in Mexico probably made him the world's richest private individual.

Nevertheless, the parts coalesced. Spanish treasure fleets united the Pacific and Atlantic seaboards to the Habsburg lands and kingdoms in Europe. New World silver sustained the wars fought by the Habsburgs in the Low Countries and Central Europe—with fleets sometimes being sent directly to Antwerp to buy off mutinous troops. From Acapulco, treasure went to Manila to be exchanged for silk, porcelain, and curiosities from the Chinese mainland. Slaves were brought from Africa to the Americas by Portuguese middlemen, mostly to serve as servants and craftsmen, although there was also demand for labour on the Caribbean and Brazilian sugar plantations. More happily, chilli pepper, tomatoes, maize corn, and chocolate enlivened the European diet. In return, the New World received the pig, the horse, and the wheel.

Coordination was not only commercial. Culturally and confessionally, the Habsburg possessions became more alike, notwithstanding their geographical separation. Religious processions and the cult of the Virgin and saints were transported westwards as part of the new traffic in souls. The pious observance of the house of Habsburg, which expressed itself in an intense veneration of the Host, spilled across the Atlantic to influence popular ritual. A new acrostic communicated the spiritual zeal of the Habsburg rulers—EUCHARISTIA, which is Latin for the Mass, but the letters of which might be rearranged to show the interconnectedness of Habsburg devotion and the global mission of the Catholic Church (hence, HIC EST AUSTRIA: 'This is Austria').

The architecture of early modern Catholicism, the baroque, was similarly impressed on the New World landscape as densely as in Central Europe. In the Austrian lands, Bohemia and, later, in Hungary, baroque facades and the characteristic onion-shaped domes were a mark of Catholic conversion. In the New World and the Philippines, the baroque also signalled the triumph of the Catholic Church over paganism, but it accommodated native traditions. It was more ornate and often embellished with traditional motifs—in the Andes with monkeys, llamas, and, in place of Christ as the Lamb of God, the guinea pig. Where missionaries confronted Buddhism, churches might also be built with verandas, for quiet contemplation.

Socially too, points of comparison may be detected. The Habsburg lands in Central Europe were largely agricultural—a condition exacerbated by the Thirty Years War, which had damaged the main industrial centres in Bohemia and Silesia. East of Vienna, the cities were shrunken and the principal commerce was in primary commodities as opposed to manufactured goods—metals, cattle, and farm produce. The peasantry were often tied to the soil and performed labour services for their lords, sometimes working on their masters' lands for three days a week. Real power rested with a landed aristocracy, many of whose members were newcomers who had risen to prominence on account of their loyalty to the ruler. Their estates were protected by the royal gift of the right of entail, which prevented them from being partitioned among heirs, and they were sustained by the fruits of office that accompanied the royal service.

In Spain, a process of 'refeudalization', beginning in the late 16th century, created analogous conditions. The towns withered and commerce became increasingly a matter of shipping the wealth of the New World into and out of Castile. An aristocracy of grandees, protected again by rights of entail, took over the properties of the crown, building up large private estates. In the countryside, four-fifths of the peasantry owned no land of their own, but either rented their farms or worked as share-croppers. The dues they owed to their lords, when combined with increasingly onerous taxation, took up roughly a half of peasant income. An expanding *hidalgo* class of petty nobles jostled for minor church offices and for employment as lawyers in the royal and local administration.

In the New World, economic and political power was increasingly concentrated in families of jointly indigenous and Spanish descent. A new *mestizo* or mixed-heritage aristocracy lived for the most part in cities like Havana and Mexico City, administering their estates and plantations at a distance, as absentee landlords. The workforce on their farms or *haciendas* and in their mines increasingly comprised servile groups, who were either obliged by the terms of their settlement to perform labour services or who had been reduced by debt to the status of bondsmen. Over time, 'debt peonage' became the condition that underpinned rural production. Conditions in the New World thus increasingly replicated those in the Old, with a wealthy aristocracy, a largely impoverished workforce, and an economy that rested on agriculture and the provision of raw materials.

The global empire of the Habsburgs came to an end in 1700. In that year, the last Habsburg ruler of Spain, Charles II, died—deranged, without heir, and habitually unkempt. For thirteen years, France and the Central European branch of the Habsburg family struggled over the Spanish succession in a war that drew in most of the European powers. But not even the triumphs of the duke of Marlborough over the French at Blenheim, Ramillies, and Oudenarde between 1704 and 1708 were sufficient to give victory to England's Habsburg ally. In a series of treaties agreed in 1714, Emperor Charles VI (1711–40) resigned his Spanish rights to the grandson of Louis XIV, who became Philip V of Spain. Charles was rewarded with the formerly Spanish possessions of Milan and the Low Countries, and

5. The Karlskirche in Vienna, commissioned by Emperor Charles VI, built 1716–37. The twin columns recall the Spanish Habsburg symbol of the Pillars of Hercules.

England with Gibraltar. Charles took with him in defeat the emblem of the Spanish Habsburgs, the Pillars of Hercules. Outside the Karlskirche church in Vienna (Figure 5), Charles erected two massive columns, each 33 metres high, in memory of the lost Habsburg inheritance of Spain and the New World.

Chapter 5
Enlightenment and reaction: 18th and 19th centuries

'Treasury science' and natural law

From the late 17th century onwards, visitors went from Habsburg Central Europe to France, England, and the Netherlands. They saw the ships, manufactures, populous cities, and energetic political discussion, all of which were missing back home. Central Europeans felt that they were backward. As one of the earliest of these self-critical observers remarked, 'We are forever only giving foreigners occasion for hearty laughter. They are laughing at us and they are right.' Or, as Philip von Hörnigk wrote in his *Austria Over All (if she only wants to)* (1684), 'Nothing is sound with us, from head to foot... Things are in such a condition that it is something like an Austrian miracle that everything has not yet gone to total ruin long ago.'

Hörnigk belonged to the group of economists known as 'cameralists' or practitioners of 'treasury science'. This was the study of how states and institutions might maximize revenues in the absence of foreign sources of enrichment and thus overcome their backwardness. Cameralists assumed that it was the purpose of the state to marshal its resources both for its own defence and for the benefit of its citizens, as a way of enlarging their wealth and happiness. The measure of this intervention differed from author to author. Some believed that it was enough to create the conditions for happiness, for it was the individual's right to determine how he reacted with the external world. Most, however, assumed that individuals could not be trusted to secure an order of maximum perfection and that a benevolent government should intervene and direct, even at the expense of individual liberty. Accordingly, cameralists frequently advocated what amounted to a 'programme of total regulation'. Within this scheme, individual rights took second place to the interests of the larger society—hence, because a burgeoning population was conceived to be good thing, abortion should be clamped down on, cripples removed from public places lest they shock women into miscarriages, and so on. The 'well-ordered' state for which the cameralists worked was sometimes called the *Polizei-Staat*, which means 'regulated state'.

Cameralism complemented the new philosophy of natural law, which by the 18th century dominated the universities and educated discussion. Natural law theory rested on two principles. The first was that society and sociability were implicit in the human condition. The second was that government existed for the benefit of society—kings did not rule because God had appointed them; their dominion was for a purpose that was located in the society of their subjects. Natural law theory gave a moral underpinning to cameralism, converting its dry economics and regulatory regime into a set of philosophical imperatives.

At its worst, cameralism and natural law could lead to a dull utilitarianism which sought to banish literature, philosophy, and astronomy from the university curriculum on the grounds that they were not 'useful'. At the other extreme, they threatened social revolution. The rights of the nobility, of their antique diets, and of the Church rested on tradition and they could hardly be justified in terms of their social benefit. They might thus be voided in the interests of the greater good. As one imperial adviser put it, 'Every tradition which has no justifiable basis should be abolished automatically.'

Theory, however, took second place to expediency. Charles VI (1711–40) had spent a good part of his reign convincing the diets and his fellow sovereigns to accept the terms of the Pragmatic Sanction of 1713. This established the indivisibility of the Habsburg lands and a single succession, including the right of daughters to inherit. Nevertheless, upon Maria Theresa's accession in 1740, Frederick the Great of Prussia seized Silesia from the young queen, contesting her right to succeed. Notwithstanding a 'diplomatic revolution', which saw the Habsburgs ally in the Seven Years War (1756–63) with France and Russia against Prussia and Britain, Maria Theresa was unable to recover more than a sliver of Silesia. Meanwhile, under Prussian rule, the main part of Silesia prospered, becoming the industrial heartland of Frederick's kingdom, despite paying increasingly burdensome taxes.

Enlightened despotism

In seeking to keep up with Prussia militarily, the Habsburgs became increasingly imitative of it. As a consequence many of the ideas which we associate with the Enlightenment were transported through the Prussian connection into Habsburg Central Europe. There they fused with the ideas of cameralism and natural law to yield a doctrine of state power. In Britain and North America, the Enlightenment tended towards the extension of popular sovereignty, curbs on government, and a new 'science of freedom' aimed at securing individual liberty and the rights of the citizen. In Central Europe, the Enlightenment tended towards the reverse—towards regulation, the 'science of the state', and the subjection of the individual to the common good, as the sovereign understood it to be. As one of the main exponents of the Central European Enlightenment put it: 'All the duties of peoples and subjects may be reduced to the formula: to promote all the ways and means adopted by the ruler for their happiness, by their obedience, fidelity and diligence.'

Maria Theresa (1740–80) and her son Joseph II (1780–90) practised a type of government that was despotic in the contemporary sense of 'ruling without due regard to established constitutions, laws and practices'. In the first decades of her reign, Maria Theresa's interest lay in administrative and military reform, the better to confront her Prussian adversary. Offices of government were merged to prevent duplication and the financial regime overhauled. State accountancy was made more rigorous, becoming one of the most sophisticated in Europe. Maria Theresa introduced conscription and personally inspected drill books and tunics. Only the light-horse hussars escaped her watch, continuing to wear haphazard items of uniform captured on the battlefield.

The diets obstructed the ruler's purpose. First, they sought to impose conditions on the taxes they voted. Secondly, they were in charge of collecting the money due, which they often did with studied incompetence. In response, Maria Theresa appointed commissions to collect the taxes agreed by the diets and sought to bind the diets to ten-year agreements on taxation. The Hungarian diet was particularly obstructive, refusing to accept Maria Theresa's proposals to limit the burdens that the nobles imposed on the peasantry. After 1765, she refused to summon it at all, but collected taxes anyway.

The kingdom of Poland was between 1772 and 1795 notoriously partitioned in three stages between Russia, Prussia, and the Habsburgs. Maria Theresa took the southernmost slice of Poland at the first partition, renaming it 'the Kingdom of Galicia and Lodomeria'. Its obscure title harked back to a time in the early 13th century when a part of the region had belonged to Hungary, on which dubious grounds Maria Theresa justified her annexation. Galicia was a testing ground. In 1775, Maria Theresa gave Galicia a new constitution, inaugurating a diet. The diet was unelected, comprising mostly churchmen and wealthy landowners. Its powers were limited to presenting petitions; in all else it was expected to defer to the ruler's demands. On those rare occasions on which it met, its sessions were confined to just a few days' deliberations.

The duchy of Milan was another arena of experiment. Milan (together with Mantua) had passed to the Central European Habsburgs in 1714, having previously belonged to the Spanish branch of the family. Maria Theresa's reform of the duchy involved the preparation of an extensive land register, which not only gave security of tenure to peasant farmers but permitted the extension of taxes onto the nobility—hitherto nobles had 'self-assessed', both concealing the extent of their own property and passing most of the burden of payment onto their tenants. An 'Economic Committee' in Milan also investigated the property and privileges of religious houses, rationalizing their number and eliminating many of the smaller houses. A similar policy was pursued in Galicia.

It is easy to explain Maria Theresa's reforms as done not in the spirit of Enlightenment but in the interests of government. In some areas she was strikingly 'unenlightened'. Believing Protestants to be potential fifth-columnists for Prussia, she maintained a vicious persecution of all those who would not take oaths of loyalty to the Catholic religion. Several thousand Protestants were deported from the Austrian lands to Transylvania. To their number, she reportedly added the loose women of Vienna, who were sent 'to the frontiers of Hungary, where they can only debauch Turks and infidels'. Maria Theresa also retained an abhorrence of Jews, communicating from behind a screen with the Jewish bankers who kept her financially afloat. Early on in her reign, Maria Theresa briefly ejected the Jewish population of Prague, at the time the largest Jewish community in Christian Europe.

Nonetheless, there were flashes of enlightened thinking, if only due to the advice Maria Theresa received from her advisers and, increasingly, her son Joseph. In 1755, she outlawed the staking of vampires, subsequently prohibiting divination and witch-hunting. As she explained, all these phenomena derived from 'silliness and ignorance which give rise to simple-minded amazement and superstitious practices'. Torture was abolished as a means of interrogation. Maria Theresa also adopted a kinder (or at least less harsh) policy towards the Gypsy population, which at this time numbered several hundreds of thousands across Central Europe. Whereas her predecessors had persecuted Gypsies and sought to expel them from the Habsburg lands, even on pain of death, Maria Theresa endeavoured to make them settled, with a view to their eventual assimilation. Even so, her policies included the forcible removal and adoption of Gypsy children, so that they might be brought up in more conventional ways.

Under Maria Theresa's son and successor, Joseph II, the pace of reform quickened. Its character was manifested in the method of its implementation, which was by decree and not through legislation made collaboratively with the diets, which were reduced to political impotence. Whereas Maria Theresa in the last decade of her reign issued on average 100 edicts a year, under her son the number rose to just under 700, or roughly two a day. Joseph ordered religious toleration in 1781 (although it did not extend to Deists, whom he deported to Transylvania), and he impressed upon the Catholic clergy that they were servants of the state not of a distant 'pope beyond the mountains'.

Joseph II placed the management of church affairs under a department of government, which controlled clerical appointments and ecclesiastical policy. He made marriage no longer a church monopoly, but permitted weddings to be conducted before magistrates. Most notoriously, in his 'Edict on Idle Institutions' he closed down monasteries which lacked schools and hospitals or provided no parish priests, putting their wealth into a fund to support religious education and clerical pensions. About a third of the monasteries in Joseph's realms were abolished. Their libraries were for the most part pulped, dumped, or abandoned to rot.

About two-and-a-half million books were destroyed in Europe's greatest biblioclasm before the Third Reich.

Joseph meddled in everything—from the length of church sermons to burial practices, like kissing the corpse, which he deemed unhygienic, and he instructed the use of reusable coffins, with false bottoms. To much derision at the time, Joseph even commissioned the preparation of wax bodies for medical schools, to be used in place of dissections. It was, however, his attempted reform of conditions on the land that aroused the greatest objections. First, Joseph abolished restrictions on the peasants, permitting them to leave the land and giving them hereditary tenures if they stayed. Then, following his mother's example in Milan, he ordered a land register with the aim of taxing the nobles and having their peasant tenants pay a proportional rent rather than perform labour services.

Joseph's measures created an outcry in Hungary, particularly since he also required all official business to be conducted there in German, for reasons of efficiency. Among the Hungarian nobility there was an upsurge in patriotic sentiment, which expressed itself in the conspicuous use of the spittoon. More seriously, conspirators made overtures to Frederick William of Prussia, even sending him books on Hungarian law so that he might acquaint himself with the rights of the nobility should he agree to replace Joseph. In the Austrian Low Countries, popular disquiet at 'the flock of edicts which attack religion' gave way in 1789 to armed insurrection and the proclamation of a 'United Belgian State'.

Joseph died in 1790, in the wake of a failed campaign against the Ottomans. On his sickbed, he withdrew his most contentious reforms. His dying wish that the epitaph on his sarcophagus should read, 'Here lies Joseph II who failed in everything he undertook', was not obeyed. It should be added that the Vienna city council also refused to implement Joseph's decree on reusable coffins. Mozart, who died shortly after Joseph, was not buried via

such a device, but in a proper coffin in a general cemetery
(and not—contrary to popular belief—in a pauper's grave).

Freemasons and Jacobins

Unhappily married, Joseph left no children—he complained that
his second wife, Maria Josepha, was so covered in boils as to make
intimacy impossible. His brother, Leopold II, thus succeeded.
Leopold engaged in a desperate work of recovery—forcing the
peasants in Bohemia back to the land, reimposing labour services,
and threatening the resentful Hungarian nobility with the partition
of their kingdom. He even restored a handful of monasteries.
Peace with the Ottomans freed up troops to bring order in
the Austrian Low Countries.

Previously as duke of Tuscany, Leopold had acquired a reputation
as an enlightened reformer. On coming to the throne in 1790,
he released political prisoners, gaoled for having disparaged
Joseph, and relaxed censorship. Joseph's index of forbidden books,
although considerably shorter than his mother's, still had works
by Goethe and Schiller among its 900 items. Leopold secretly
enlisted enthusiasts for the French Revolution to pamphleteer
against the institution of nobility, the more to make the nobles
cleave to the monarch for safety. Meanwhile, Leopold plotted
military intervention in France to support his brother-in-law,
the beleaguered Louis XVI.

The outcome was predictable—a war with France, which made the
Austrian Low Countries a battlefield, and the conversion of
the paid hacks of revolution into genuine revolutionaries. By this
time, Leopold was dead, so it fell to his son Francis to face the
consequences of his policies.

During the last decades of the 18th century, Vienna had acquired
'a public sphere'. Beer halls, coffee shops, and the popular theatre
provided venues for discussion and political criticism. On stage,

the harlequin Jack Sausage ('Hanswurst') poked ribald fun at ministers. Despite the censorship, foreign newspapers circulated and were read out in coffee houses, where as one police report explained, there were 'more and more conversations that are as insulting to the sovereign as they are to religion and morals'.

Amongst the small number of the educated, freemasonry was common. By the 1780s, there were no less than sixteen lodges in Vienna, which were in correspondence with 300 lodges across Europe, from London to St Petersburg. Joseph II was never a freemason, regarding its rites as foolish, but a number of his advisers were, with several being admitted through the so-called 'Scottish rite' to the higher and more arcane degrees. In Bohemia, freemasonry captured many of the foremost aristocrats, while at least two abbots of the great Benedictine abbey of Melk were buried in masonic aprons.

Freemasonry's rituals had nothing to do with revolution. The protocols of the Eternal Harmony Lodge in Vienna list the lectures given there, which were mostly edifying talks on freemasonic lore—'Secrets of the Egyptians', 'Was Christ a freemason?', and so on. Doubtless, those of a rebellious disposition found kindred souls in the lodges. The administrative practices of freemasonry—writing constitutions and agendas, organizing rules of debate, and taking minutes—might also be harnessed to political organization.

Outside the lodges, the former protégés of Leopold II talked revolution. Some opened up channels to the French and plotted insurrection, but their activity was mostly given over to absurd plans and vulgar ditties:

> The people aren't just bog roll, but can do their own thinking.
> If you won't learn good manners, you'll be hanged like a lout.
> Off to the guillotine, blood for blood.
> Had we a guillotine here, a lot of big guys would pay.

One of the earliest plots involved the distribution of proclamations by '100,000 specially trained dogs' (even the authorities refused to take it seriously). Another included the construction of a war-machine of pikes mounted around an axle, for use by peasants against cavalry. Since the conspirators had no links whatever to the countryside, it was never built, let alone tested.

Military defeat, conscription, and food shortages might, nonetheless, create the circumstances for revolution. Police reports reaching the government exaggerated the potential for unrest, confusing 'the itch to criticize' with dissidence. In 1794, several score of the more prominent 'Jacobins' were arrested and put on trial. There was one execution in Vienna, and seven in Hungary. Most of those tried were either found not guilty or pardoned. The long prison terms given to the remainder were subsequently commuted.

The significance of the Jacobin trials was larger than the paltry threat posed by the conspirators. Throughout Europe, it was feared that revolution might be exported from France—even England suspended *Habeas Corpus* in 1794. The Jacobin trials proved that there was plotting of some sort going on. They justified the extension of the criminal law to include 'impudent criticism', the closing of all masonic lodges, the tightening of censorship to include mottoes on fans and snuffboxes, and the recruitment of informers. The improvised stage-routines of Jack Sausage were now forbidden. The Habsburg lands turned inwards and most plans for reform were from the mid-1790s abandoned as politically dangerous. The better-off and educated settled into the domesticity of the 'Biedermeier' (so called after a fictional petit bourgeois), with its bright waistcoats, pigeonhole desks, and Schubert *Lieder*.

Metternich

Between 1792 and 1814, the Habsburgs were at war with France for a total period of 108 months and they were engaged on land against Napoleon for an even longer period than Great Britain. Habsburg participation in four of the first five coalitions formed against France between 1793 and 1809 proved disastrous. Vienna was twice occupied by French forces. Step by step, the Habsburgs were stripped of their territories. Belgium (the former Austrian Low Countries), Further Austria, Milan, and the Tyrol had all gone by 1805. Four years later, Napoleon joined together parts of Croatia, Carniola, and the Habsburg territories on the Adriatic coast to make the Illyrian Provinces, which were declared a part of France. Francis's daughter was married off to the Corsican commoner who had impudently declared himself an emperor. Even she was a conspicuous second best, for Tsar Alexander of Russia had previously refused Napoleon his own daughter.

In 1809, Clemens von Metternich took direction of Habsburg foreign policy, at the lowest point in its fortunes. Metternich was a coifed dandy, an elegant 'Adonis of the salons', given to fits of histrionics. An astute but smooth career diplomat, who had previously bedded Napoleon's sister, he got on sufficiently well with Napoleon for him to disclose his plans for war with Russia. Metternich discerned that Napoleon had underestimated 'the vast space' involved.

On Metternich's advice, Francis joined in the French attack on Russia in 1812 as an 'armed neutral', sending only a token force. Then, following Napoleon's disastrous defeat, Francis threw in his lot with the Sixth Coalition. At the Battle of Leipzig fought in 1813, the Habsburg armies contributed almost a third of the victorious coalition forces. The next year, the allies were in Paris and the French monarchy was restored.

The international settlement that concluded the Napoleonic Wars met in Vienna in 1814–15. It continued its deliberations right through the 'Hundred Days', which saw Napoleon escape from exile to meet his final defeat at Waterloo. The Congress of Vienna was chaired by Metternich and resulted in modest gains for the Habsburgs. The Tyrol and Milan were returned, and augmented by Venice and its Adriatic possessions, including Istria and Dalmatia, and by Salzburg, previously ruled by its archbishop. The Congress did not restore the Holy Roman Empire, abolished in 1806, but put in its place a loose German Confederation under Habsburg presidency. The title of Francis as emperor of Austria was acknowledged, on account of which we may now properly speak of an Austrian or Habsburg Empire.

Metternich dominated Habsburg foreign policy until 1848 and he exercised a major influence in domestic affairs too. He always explained his diplomatic objectives in terms of a 'balance of power' and maintaining an equilibrium, but behind these clichés lay his fear of a revived France. The experience of the French wars had shown that the Habsburg Empire was not able to confront France except as part of an alliance and that it was now in the second rank of Great Powers, behind Russia and Britain. At the same time, Metternich discerned a continuing revolutionary impulse, which threatened stability across Europe. Influenced by the earlier fear of Jacobinism, he believed revolutionary politics to be coordinated by a secret committee in Paris, which fomented across Europe a network of conspiracies. Accordingly, he promoted regular meetings of representatives of Europe's major states with the aim of securing joint intervention abroad in favour of the status quo and of keeping France, 'the great factory of revolution', in its place.

The Concert of Europe's foremost states soon ceased to convene. Its members could not agree and they lacked both the will and muscle to police all of Europe. Metternich thus acted alone. In the early 1830s, he occupied parts of Italy in order to restore their rulers and, in 1846, he annexed the Free City of Cracow. Cracow had been established as a protectorate by the Congress of Vienna, but Metternich used its complicity in an insurrection in Galicia to justify its seizure. He also used Austria's presidency of the German

Confederation to push through decrees aimed at curbing student radicalism and censoring the press.

Metternich's interest in stemming revolutionary activity abroad derived from his fear that revolution would spill over into the Habsburg Empire, reawakening the plotting of the 1790s. It may well be that he was misguided. Nonetheless, there were powerful and popular insurrectionary movements in Habsburg Italy and Galicia, while disturbances in the Hungarian countryside might easily be mistaken for sedition. Even so, the censorship practised in the Habsburg Empire was light and as much concerned with moral sensibilities as political opinions. Nor did it affect publications longer than 300 pages, since these were deemed too tiring for readers and censors alike. The number of political prisoners was never more than a few dozen, and some of them were plainly guilty of plotting violence.

Metternich's influence under Emperor Francis was limited by the ruler's immobility, for Francis preferred the safety of inaction to the unpredictability of change. In 1835, Francis died and was succeeded by his son, Ferdinand (Figure 6). Unusually proportioned and eccentric, the new emperor left the affairs of state to a council of regency while he busied with the classification of plants. The council was nominally headed by Ferdinand's brother, Archduke Ludwig, but Metternich was the main force within it.

Metternich is frequently described as a conservative, who by his failure to reform the Habsburg Empire left it open to the very revolution he feared. As the British Foreign Secretary, Lord Palmerston, warned, 'Your repressive and suffocating policy is also a fatal one and will lead to an explosion.' Despite his reputation, Metternich was not opposed to modest change. Within the council of regency and the bureaucracy were supporters of Joseph II's policies and Metternich encouraged their schemes to improve the economy. By this time, however, cameralist ideas of state intervention had given way to the laissez-faire of Smith and

6. Ferdinand I of Habsburg in retirement in Prague, *c.*1870. A keen botanist, the genus *Ferdinandusa* was named in his honour. He retained even after his abdication in 1848 the title of 'His Majesty, the Emperor'. Portraits composed during his reign concealed the deformity of his skull, which was the result of childhood rickets.

Ricardo. So regulation was now used to deregulate, removing impediments to commerce and factories, abolishing some of the last privileges of the guilds, and eliminating many tariffs and tolls. Industrial production and railway-building burgeoned and, along with it, rapid urbanization. Vienna's population swelled from 230,000 in 1800 to 430,000 in 1848. Notwithstanding further relaxation of the marriage laws, the number of illegitimate births in the capital rose to two in every five.

Social policy lagged behind and Metternich made little attempt to address the condition of the peasantry or to manage the economic distress which periodically affected the cities, particularly after the crop failures of the mid-1840s. Nor did he build enduring political alliances at home, preferring temporary agreements and accommodations, which when they came unstuck often froze policy-making. He did nothing to repair the institutions of government, particularly at a provincial level. The diets thus remained unreformed, even though they were the only bodies that had any sort of representative character. The Upper Austrian diet met for only three hours a year, to nod through whatever was put before it. Its Transylvanian and Hungarian counterparts were livelier, but when the diets voiced unwelcome demands Metternich ordered them closed and arrested their noisiest members. Metternich feared that the diets would push for changes that would contain the seeds of revolution. As Palmerston had foreseen, however, Metternich's aversion to political reform only made revolution more likely.

Chapter 6
The era of Franz Joseph: 19th century

The revolutionary year

On the evening of 13 March 1848, Metternich was asked by
Archduke Ludwig to resign, which he did reluctantly. Close to the
palace in Vienna, the street lights had been torn up and the gas
pipes lit at pavement level, sending jets of flame skyward. Patrols
of students and citizens had taken over the task of maintaining
order from the military. There was looting in the suburbs, but in
the centre of the city crowds eerily massed to cheer the emperor.
Metternich fled Vienna that night, reputedly in female disguise,
taking the train to London.

The revolution that forced Metternich out was one of many in
Europe in 1848. From February onwards, in Italy and then
in France and across the German Confederation, governments
were overthrown under pressure from the streets. To that extent,
what happened in Vienna was expected.

The revolution in Vienna originated in demonstrations that
mimicked the previous month's events in Paris. In the ensuing
tumult, self-appointed spokesmen put forward modest
programmes of reform. The first demand was the relaxation of
censorship. Then, ideas of a constitution, political representation,
and social reform were added to the mix. On 15 March Emperor

Ferdinand, acting on the advice of a new government, formally declared censorship abolished, promised to convene reformed diets, and committed himself to a constitution. Overnight, booksellers moved their hidden stocks of banned publications into shop windows.

The events in Vienna resounded throughout the Empire. Over the last decades, many of the ideas of liberalism, with its stress on the rule of law, political representation, and the rights of the citizen, had acquired a following. So too had nationalism, which emphasized the nation. The idea of the nation was at this time based mainly on language and, to a lesser extent, on religion. Although intellectually opposed, liberal individualism and nationalist collectivism worked together. The universalism of the reformers' demands was demonstrated in the students' flag, which adopted the colours of the rainbow.

During the spring and early summer of 1848, the government published a constitution and an imperial parliament or Reichstag, elected on a wide franchise, gathered in July. By this time, however, an elected assembly, which included representatives from the Austrian lands, was also meeting in Frankfurt to work out a constitution for a new Germany. In Hungary, a separate government was installed, with the emperor's consent. Meanwhile, a self-appointed 'Pan-Slav' Congress convened in Prague to represent Slavonic speakers from across the empire—Czechs, Slovaks, Poles, Ukrainians, and so on—with the aim of building 'a confederation of nations'. In Transylvania, Romanians and Germans demanded self-rule, while the Croats sought to establish a government in Zagreb that was no longer under Hungarian control.

The danger was that the Habsburg Empire would be broken up. Its German-speaking Austrian parts would join a new Germany, while Bohemia formed the core of a new Slav state. A greatly reduced Hungary would then become an independent kingdom, with an archipelago of new states on its edge. None of this could be achieved, however, except through civil war. In a hint of things to come, King Charles Albert of Piedmont, who aimed to create a unified Italian state in the north of the peninsula, occupied Habsburg Milan and made common cause with Venice, which had declared an independent republic. By the middle of 1848, it looked as if the dissolution of the Habsburg Empire was certain.

The government in Vienna, presided over by a succession of reluctant prime ministers, had lost control of events, and so the initiative passed to the generals. At some point in May, the Minister of War, Count Latour, gave the go-ahead for military action. He did so without reference to the emperor or to the other ministers in Vienna. Following Latour's lead, Field Marshal Radetzky in Italy ignored previous instructions to keep his troops in barracks, and defeated Charles Albert in a series of engagements in June and July. His victories were celebrated in Vienna with the elder Johann Strauss's composition 'The Radetzky March'. Radetzky went on to besiege Venice, where he later deployed balloons loaded with explosive against the city. Meanwhile in June, Field Marshal Windischgrätz held manoeuvres outside Prague. When these prompted violent demonstrations, he bombarded the city into submission and dispersed the Pan-Slav Congress. He then turned his attention to Vienna.

Conditions in Vienna were increasingly chaotic. The main park was crowded with unemployed labourers and idlers who collected the poor relief distributed there in return for doing useless 'public work'. Twenty thousand ended up camping in the park, issuing out at night to rob and loot. A radicalized press taunted enemies of the revolution, and government ministers were kept awake at night by 'caterwauling', done by gangs howling and screeching violin strings outside their homes. Caterwauling (*Katzenmusik*) spread to other Austrian cities, where it claimed the life of the 'real' Baron Frankenstein, who was the inventor of electro-plating and a pioneer of photography, but known to be a government sympathizer. Driven to despair by the racket outside his house, he either killed himself or had a heart attack. Another victim was Count Latour, who was hanged by a Viennese mob from a lamp post.

Windischgrätz's campaign against Vienna is a textbook illustration on how to subdue a city. First, he evacuated the imperial family and, along with it, the Reichstag that had spent the previous months in earnest debate, mostly over the terms of the peasantry's emancipation. Both were moved to Moravia. Then the garrison was withdrawn. On 29 October, Windischgrätz distributed a proclamation warning that he would begin bombardment the next day. A flight of citizens left only the most dangerous revolutionaries and troublemakers within. After five days of fighting, Windischgrätz captured the city.

Government and constitutions

Hungary was unsubdued. In April 1848, Emperor Ferdinand had sanctioned the April Laws, originally drafted by the Hungarian diet, which had established a government in Hungary with extensive powers of self-rule. Over the next six months, the Hungarian government sought to make good its rights and more, establishing an army, printing a new currency, and conducting its own foreign relations. Although Hungary declared itself independent only in April 1849, it had for the preceding year been effectively operating its own policies, with minimal reference to the government in Vienna.

The Hungarian kingdom was by no means unified nationally. Hungarian-speakers made up less than a half of the population. The others were Croats, Slovaks, Serbs, Germans, Ukrainians, and Romanians. These now rebelled against the government in Buda in a multi-faceted struggle that in the Banat also pitted Romanians against Serbs. For this, the intransigence of the Hungarian government was partly to blame, for it paid little heed to the aspirations of Hungary's smaller nations. The government in Vienna, however, fanned dissent, supporting the invasion of Hungary by a Croatian army.

To settle the affairs of Hungary, Emperor Ferdinand had to go, for he was compromised by having agreed in the first place to the April Laws. This was the conviction of Prince Schwarzenberg, the new Prime Minister appointed in November. Schwarzenberg was closely linked to Radetzky, to Windischgrätz, who was his brother-in-law, and to the Croatian commander Josip Jellačić—and the generals were now setting the political pace. Satirical pamphlets published in Vienna played on the imperial 'We'—WIR, now standing for Windischgrätz, Jellačić, and Radetzky.

The emperor's entourage, having abandoned Vienna, was resident in the Moravian city of Olomouc. Its members received at short notice an invitation to attend on 2 December the archbishop's palace, where the imperial family was staying. There, in the audience chamber, they witnessed what amounted to a military coup. First, Emperor Ferdinand formally abdicated, which he did with good grace; then, the next in line to the throne, his feeble brother Franz Karl, gave up his rights at the insistence of his wife. The mantle thus passed, literally, to Franz Karl's son, the 18-year-old Franz Joseph. A surviving watercolour shows the teenager being led forward by his mother and aunt, with Ferdinand and Franz Karl in the background. Around an improvised throne stand Schwarzenberg, Jellačić, and Windischgrätz (Figure 7). (Ferdinand subsequently retired to Prague, to continue his botanical interests. He died in 1875.)

The suppression of Hungary was slow and brutal. The generals were outmanoeuvred by the brilliance of the Hungarian commanders and by the organizational genius and charisma of the Hungarian political leader, Louis Kossuth. It was only in the summer of 1849 that the Habsburg army, acting in concert

7. Franz Joseph is conducted to the throne, 2 December 1848. Watercolour by Leopold Kupelwieser. Left to right: Archduke Franz Karl, Emperor Ferdinand, Empress Maria Anna, Franz Joseph, Princess Sophie, Prince Schwarzenberg, Field Marshal Windischgrätz, and General Jellačić.

with Russian troops, put an end to the Hungarian war for independence. In retribution, Franz Joseph ordered the hanging of thirteen Hungarian generals and of a former Hungarian Prime Minister. As one former Habsburg minister put it, the new emperor had inaugurated his reign with 'the scaffold and the bloodbath'.

Franz Joseph had closed down in 1849 the Reichstag that had been meeting in Moravia. Even so, with the revolutions crushed he posed for a brief period as a constitutionalist, making ostentatious plans for a new assembly in which all parts of the Habsburg Empire would be represented. By adopting the pretence of constitutionalism, he hoped to win over the German princes to the idea of an 'empire of seventy millions', which would combine the German Confederation and Habsburg Empire in a loose political and economic union. When it became clear that the smaller German states would not fall into line, Franz Joseph dropped his mask and at the end of 1851 embarked upon sole rule. For almost a decade, he summoned neither a parliament nor the provincial diets. The regime he headed was typified by his great uncle, Archduke Albrecht, the governor of Hungary. Asked by a group of Hungarian aristocrats to help restore Hungary's constitution, Albrecht waved his sword at them, exclaiming, 'This is my constitution'.

The nine years of 'neo-absolutism' resemble Joseph II's reign, except that Franz Joseph's vision was narrower. German was once more instituted as the official language throughout the Empire, and legislation made by decree. The Catholic Church, however, was restored to its privileges and the right to civil marriage restricted in respect of 'mixed' unions between Catholics and non-Catholics. The police cracked down on dissent and the press, and the courts exacted harsh penalties for petty political transgressions—wearing cockades in provocative colours, penning satirical verses, and so on. More positively, a customs union between Hungary and the rest of the Empire generated economic growth. In 1848, restrictions on the peasantry had been abolished throughout the Empire and the lands they had tilled were now made their own. But no mechanisms had been established to work out what lands the peasants were entitled to. This was now done, and small compensation paid to landlords.

The problem was finance. The unaccountability of Franz Joseph's regime discouraged the bankers from lending to it at a time when the annual deficit amounted to a half of state income. The army was accordingly left ill equipped and badly trained—much of its complement was on semi-permanent leave anyway. The cost of war meant that the Habsburg Empire did not intervene in the Crimea in 1853 to halt Russian expansion. Then, in 1859, Franz Joseph's armies were worsted by the French in Italy. Milan was lost to France's protégé, the king of Piedmont, to whom Venice was also later surrendered. Without money from the bankers and political reform, one minister warned, the entire future of the Empire was in jeopardy.

Franz Joseph abandoned neo-absolutism grudgingly, first instituting an advisory ministerial council and then expanding its membership to include hand-picked representatives of the provincial diets, which were accordingly restored. When these half-hearted measures failed to restore confidence, he went the whole way. In February 1861, Franz Joseph ordered the establishment of a two-chamber parliament or Reichsrat. The upper house would comprise heads of noble families, churchmen, and Habsburg archdukes; the lower would comprise elected representatives, originally drawn from the diets. In 1867, he agreed to a Settlement or 'Compromise' with Hungary, giving the kingdom its own government and parliament, with an Upper House of dignitaries and an elected Lower House. To satisfy Hungarian demands, Transylvania was now absorbed into Hungary, thus putting an end to the separate existence it had enjoyed for more than three centuries. The Settlement was partly forced upon Franz Joseph by foreign policy concerns. The Habsburg struggle with Prussia over leadership in Germany, which was marked by a brief but decisive war in 1866, required peaceful conditions at home and an accommodation with the Hungarians.

In 1867, Franz Joseph published constitutions for both the Austrian and Hungarian halves of the Empire. They embedded the rule of law and parliamentary rights, and were duly adopted by the two parliaments. From this point onwards, the Habsburg Empire comprised two constitutionally equal parts—a Hungarian part and a part for all the rest. The second had no obvious name and was officially known as 'The Lands and Kingdoms Represented in the Reichsrat' and unofficially as 'This side of the Leitha' (Cis-Leithania: the River Leitha marked the border between the two entities). In combination, the Empire became Austria-Hungary, the Dual Monarchy, or the Austro-Hungarian Empire. Austria only became the official name of the non-Hungarian half in 1915.

The Habsburg Empire (see Map 2) now had parliaments and 'this side of the Leitha' it also had elected diets, but its government was not parliamentary. The governments in both halves of the Empire were responsible to the emperor and not to the parliaments in Vienna and Budapest (the cities of Pest and Buda were amalgamated in 1873). So, it was quite possible for governments to survive votes of no confidence, providing they had the emperor's support. The emperor conducted his own foreign policy and military deployments, with minimal parliamentary oversight. Franz Joseph also had the right to legislate by decree, again with few constraints, which meant that he could bypass or substitute for the parliamentary process. On account of its intractability, Franz Joseph closed down the parliament in Vienna in March 1914. It did not reassemble for more than three years. For much of the time, however, Franz Joseph impressed his will by hard work. At his desk by no later than 5.00 a.m., he was better informed than any minister or politician.

During the first decades of his rule, Franz Joseph had a reputation for ruthlessness and even cruelty, as well as for unsoundness of judgement. The British attaché in Vienna reported in 1852 how the emperor had insisted upon a parade during a hard frost, despite being warned of the danger, with the consequence that the horses toppled over, killing two cuirassiers. In 1854, Franz Joseph married Elisabeth (Sisi) of Bavaria. Theirs was not a happy marriage. Franz Joseph continued to have mistresses, either procured on his behalf or personally chanced upon while promenading in the gardens of the Schönbrunn summer palace. He had a preference for married women, with a home to go to, the husbands having been paid off. The empress travelled, often in her later years to the Achilleion Palace on Corfu, where she retains the distinction of being the only person whose attempts at interior

Map 2. The Habsburg Empire 1873.

decoration were improved upon by the German emperor, Wilhelm II, who owned the palace after her. Sisi was also a frequent visitor to Hungary. The affection in which Sisi was held by Hungarians (a sentiment which remains to this day) helped overcome the ill will towards the Habsburgs which her husband's suppression of the country had engendered.

The misfortunes of Franz Joseph's personal life did, however, elicit over time a wider public sympathy for him. In 1867, his brother Maximilian was executed by republican forces in Mexico, who were opposed to his rule there as the emperor imposed on the country by the French and the Mexican landowners. In 1898, the empress was killed by an Italian anarchist in Geneva. Her murder came only a few years after the death of Franz Joseph's only son and heir, Rudolf. Rudolf's suicide, done in a murderous pact with his mistress (she was not the first whom Rudolf invited to join him in death), was concealed at the time, but was widely suspected. On account of Rudolf's suicide, Franz Joseph's nephew, Franz Ferdinand, became heir-presumptive.

Nationalism

Nationality was one of the ways by which the peoples of the Habsburg Empire made sense of their world. National identities were not clear cut until around the middle of the 19th century. Before then, many Slovaks thought of themselves as 'Slavonic Hungarians', while in the Banat, some Romanians embraced the description of 'Romanian-speaking Hungarians'. Groups acquired and lost identities. The Winds (or Windisch) of Carniola merged into the duchy's Slovene majority—only those who had previously emigrated to the American Midwest retained their old name. Individual German-speakers in the Austrian lands, Bohemia, and Transylvania might embrace a larger 'Pan-German' identity or, aware of their own cultural specificities and history, a regional one. Within families, identities sometimes competed.

Louis Kossuth led the Hungarians in their war of independence, but his uncle was a notable Slovak patriot.

Language was the main badge of identity and government censuses required everyone to declare a single linguistic affiliation. Repeated every decade after 1869, the census-takers made all citizens tick off which language they used 'in conversation' (in Hungary, their 'mother tongue'). Eight languages were given, including 'Czech-Moravian-Slovak', but omitting the many local languages that were actually in use (Lemko, Yiddish, Pulsch, and so on). Nor did the census recognize that people might use several languages, the choice of which depended on context. One soldier's diary from around 1900 was, for instance, written in four languages—in the soldier's local Slovene when he was recalling his girlfriend, in German for regimental matters, in Serbian when he composed songs, and in Hungarian when he related his sexual fantasies. The censuses, however, impressed the idea that people had a single linguistic and cultural identity, which might be classified and counted. Ethnic cartographers likewise marshalled peoples into blocks, obscuring the nuances of belonging behind diagonal and hatched lines.

Identities once impressed acquired potency. Everything became national—from the newspaper read aloud in the tavern, to items of dress and the shape of a man's moustache. One diligent observer counted twenty-three varieties of moustache, each of which signalled a national affiliation of some sort. Alcohol was another mark—Hungarian patriots drank wine; the Slovak peasantry brandy. The marks of identity were mostly masculine. In the collective rituals of belonging, often performed around statues, the female role was largely confined to girls in white holding flowers.

In most of the lands and kingdoms of the Habsburg Empire, the populations were mixed between nationalities, each of which was increasingly conscious of its separate identity. Nationalism engendered its own rivalries and performances. In Bohemian towns, Czechs and Germans had separate volunteer fire brigades, which raced each other to put out conflagrations. The university in Prague was also broken up into separate German and Czech foundations—only the botanical garden was common to both, for the names of the plants were given there in Latin. In the tiny Adriatic County of Görz-Gradisca, the main railway station was left unnamed, since Slovenes and Italians disagreed on the spelling. In Bohemian cities, fisticuffs were common enough as Czechs and Germans sought to carve out national spaces, demarcating them with statues honouring the relevant national heroes. For the most part, however, violence was rare and seldom lethal. Franz Joseph's empire had no Ireland.

The parliaments in both halves of the Empire were elected. In Hungary, the vote belonged only to the wealthy, which was intended to disenfranchise the national minorities, whose members were generally too poor to qualify. Only one in four adult males had the vote in Hungary and in Croatia one in twenty. Most Hungarian constituencies retained open voting, the better to manipulate the outcome. In the other half of the Empire, the vote was steadily extended to include by 1907 most adult males. This was done in the expectation that the lower orders would return conservative candidates to the Reichsrat. They generally did so, and although there were subsequently gains for the Socialists, their party split on national lines in 1910. Agrarian parties representing the interests of the better-off rural population never united to form a common block. Nor did the Christian Social parties, otherwise united by their allegiance to Catholicism and to programmes that were both anti-big business and anti-socialist, manage to overcome their national differences.

With thirty parties in contention, divided by both national affiliation and ideology, political stalemate prevailed in the Reichsrat. Disputes over the language to be used in the Bohemian postal service or the admissions policy in Styrian schools resulted in uproar, with ink pots being hurled and chairs overturned. This suited Franz Joseph. In the absence of a concerted political opposition, he could direct the affairs of the Empire, muddling through the daily inconveniencies of democracy by, as one Prime Minister explained, 'keeping the nationalities in a condition of even and well-modulated discontent'. On those occasions when political management failed, the emperor closed down the parliament and ruled temporarily by decree, waiting for tempers to cool. Political paralysis resulted in sensible and necessary measures, such as the funding of the army and the coordination of the budgets in both halves of the Empire, being either blocked or delayed.

Nevertheless, a solution of some sort was found, which roughly corresponds to what social scientists call 'asymmetrical federalization'—that is, power was distributed unevenly, but in such a way as to prevent a total breakdown. In Hungary, political hegemony was given to the so-called Liberals, who acted on behalf of the Hungarian-speakers or Magyars. The Liberals pursued a discriminatory national policy, closing down the schools and cultural associations of the lesser nationalities—principally, Slovaks, Romanians, and Serbs. The Hungarian policy of 'Magyarization' proved not only ineffective but also aroused international condemnation.

The Poles in Galicia practised a national supremacy similar to the Magyars, the majority of Ruthenes (Ukrainians) being disenfranchised. In Carniola, Slovenes assumed control of the local parliament and government, largely ousting the small German minority from influence. In Dalmatia, Habsburg policy favoured the Croat majority over the traditional Italian ruling elite, but not to the extent that Dalmatia was permitted to join together with Croatia. Bohemia, however, was divided roughly two to one between Czechs and Germans, with many Germans living around the border in the so-called Sudetenland. The Germans were accordingly given devolved powers, which allowed them control of those localities where they were in the majority. Jobs in the bureaucracy were duplicated in Bohemia to keep both Czechs and Germans happily in salaries. By 1900 there were more civil servants in Prague than in London, including the British colonial administration.

Vienna, the *fin de siècle*, and Jews

Vienna at the close of the 19th and in the early 20th century is most associated with the lavish avant-garde paintings of Gustav Klimt. Vienna was more than this, for it was also the city that produced Sigmund Freud, Ludwig Wittgenstein, the architect Adolf Loos, Arnold Schoenberg, the leader of the 20th century's musical revolution, and Karl Renner and Otto Bauer, who made revolutionary Marxism compatible with the salon. The explosion of artistic and intellectual vitality that took place around the end of the 19th century (hence *fin de siècle*) was not unique to Vienna—there were equal efflorescences in Paris, Berlin, and Dublin. What made Vienna exceptional was its low cultural starting point. Hitherto its reputation had been almost exclusively for music, and principally for the classical composition of Mozart, Haydn, and Beethoven.

Many of the prominent figures in *fin-de-siècle* Vienna were of Jewish descent. Besides Freud, Wittgenstein, Schoenberg, and Bauer, they include Gustav Mahler, the writers and dramatists Hofmannsthal and Schnitzler, and the two scholars who transformed the study of economics and law, Ludwig von Mises and Hans Kelsen. Others, like Klimt, Kokoschka, Schiele, and Loos, were not Jewish, and the Jewish contribution in art and architecture was less than in other fields. Even so, the gallery-owners, dealers, and patrons of artists were often Jewish, as were the subjects of several of Klimt's most famous portraits.

Central European Jewry was more numerous than in Western Europe. Its population stood in the mid-18th century at around 150,000 in the Austrian lands, Bohemia, and Hungary.

The acquisition of Galicia in 1772 brought with it a further 200,000 persons. The small province of Bukovina, obtained two years later, which lay to the east of Galicia, also had a burgeoning Jewish population, enlarged by immigration from Russia. The capital of Bukovina, Czernowitz (Chernivtsi, now in Ukraine), which was one-third Jewish in 1900, became one of the great centres of Central European Jewish culture, including the Yiddish theatre.

Most Jews in the Habsburg lands were *Landesjuden*, who worked in the countryside or on crown estates. In order to render Jews 'more useful and serviceable to the State', Joseph II removed many of the disabilities which hindered their social and economic advancement. Emancipation coincided with the Jewish 'Haskalah' or Enlightenment which stressed secular values and the importance of integration.

There were several Jewish 'paths to modernity', through ennoblement and state service, manufacturing and commerce, the professions, and later on emigration. Assimilationist strategies were rejected in large parts of Galicia, where Hassidism stressed fidelity to Talmudic traditions. Elsewhere, however, Jews abandoned the countryside for integration and advancement in the cities. By the 1880s, 10 per cent of the population of Vienna was Jewish. In Budapest, the proportion was higher still, exceeding 20 per cent in 1910.

Jews dominated the professions in Vienna, making up three-quarters of the lawyers and a half of medical doctors. They also constituted a significant part of the educated middle class—roughly a third of all grammar school (*Gymnasien*) students were Jewish. Middle-class values of rationalism and progress, however, were under assault from the banalities of daily nationalism. The election in Vienna of Europe's first antisemitic mayor, Karl Lueger, in 1895, indicated the limits of Jewish integration. It was partly the rise of antisemitism in Vienna that prompted the journalist Theodor Herzl to embrace the idea of establishing a

Jewish state in the Land of Israel. The Vienna of Klimt was also the Vienna of the young Adolf Hitler.

It may well be that under these circumstances Jews and other disillusioned members of the educated middle class in Vienna retreated into an 'aesthetic temple of art', but the proposition cannot be tested conclusively. What is certain is that cultural creativity in Vienna was strongly non-national. If anything, its interest in sexuality and the erotic looked beyond nationalism into the deeper impulses that guided human behaviour.

Nonetheless, the cosmopolitan content of Viennese *fin-de-siècle* culture was understood as one way out of the nationalist political impasse. As one exponent of the Vienna avant-garde (Berta Szeps-Zuckerkandl) put it at the time, the task of the artist was to work towards 'a purely Austrian culture that would weld together all the characteristics of our multitude of constituent peoples into a new and proud unity'. Government was not slow to see the opportunity, founding an Arts Council in 1899 to promote new cultural ideas. Shortly afterwards, the Minister of Culture described how 'works of art speak a common language and…lead to mutual understanding and reciprocal respect'.

Elsewhere in the Empire, art and culture forsook the aesthetic temple for the workshop of nationalism, seeking out artistic forms that glorified national traditions. In Budapest, Árpád Feszty painted a 120-metre cyclorama depicting the Hungarian Conquest of the 9th century—it remains to this day compulsory viewing for Hungarian schoolchildren. In Prague, Alphonse Mucha produced a rival masterpiece, comprising twenty enormous canvases that depicted mythological episodes in Czech and Slavic history. In architecture, Ödön Lechner, 'the Hungarian Gaudí', used folkloristic motifs to decorate museums, schools, and even the Budapest municipal post office, while in his designs for Budapest Zoo, Károly Kós used architectural styles familiar from the Hungarian countryside (Figure 8). Budapest's best-known

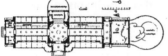

8. Design for the Aviary in Budapest Zoo, by Károly Kós, 1909. The design is based on some traditional Hungarian churches in Transylvania.

building, its Gothic parliament, embodied the national aspiration to have its representative institutions accorded the same respect as the British parliament and the Palace of Westminster.

Franz Csokor's drama *3 November 1918* premièred in Vienna in 1937. In one scene, soldiers gather to bury their colonel, who has shot himself upon news of the Empire's collapse. They each heap soil upon his corpse—'earth from Hungary...earth from Carinthia...Czech earth', symbolically burying the Empire with him. The colonel's Jewish comrade is last, stuttering, 'Earth from, earth from...Austria.' We may question the extent and contribution of Jews to *fin-de-siècle* culture. Nevertheless, Jews in Vienna stood for something larger than the nation and they may come closest to an 'Austrian idea' that transcended nationalism. By 1914, however, that idea was fast running out.

Chapter 7

World war and dissolution: 20th century

Bosnia-Herzegovina

International politics in the later 19th and early 20th centuries was dominated by the 'Eastern Question'. This was the question of what to do with the crumbling Ottoman Empire's possessions in the Balkans and how to accommodate the aspirations of the peoples under Turkish rule. The Habsburg Empire had little interest in advancing southwards. The problem was that Russia did, threatening to outflank the Habsburg Empire. The tsars of Russia saw themselves as the champions of the Orthodox Slav population of the Balkans, but they also aimed to control the straits at Istanbul that joined the Black Sea to the Mediterranean.

During the 1870s, Russia supported revolts in the Balkans against Turkish rule and attempted to establish a puppet Bulgarian state that embraced half of the peninsula. International mediation at the 1878 Congress of Berlin put a temporary end to Russian ambitions. Although Bulgaria survived, its territory was much reduced and it received a German prince as sovereign. In order to shore up the western Balkans against internal collapse, the Turkish province of Bosnia-Herzegovina was placed in 1878 under Habsburg military occupation, although it remained in name a part of the Ottoman Empire.

Habsburg rule in Bosnia-Herzegovina was not confined to garrisoning. The province was given schools, hospitals, a measure of local government, and an efficient administration, although it was not until 1910 that it had its own elected parliament. Viennese architecture was combined with local folkloric motifs to deliver a 'Bosnian style', which transformed the centre of the capital city of Sarajevo. Most spectacularly, the Habsburg administration in Bosnia-Herzegovina laid down more than 1,000 kilometres of railway track. The North Bosnian line, which ran through mountainous terrain east of Sarajevo, included 99 tunnels and 30 iron bridges in a stretch of just 160 kilometres. The so-called 'Bosnian narrow gauge' (of 760 mm) subsequently became an international benchmark and was adopted across Europe as well as in the Congo and Argentina. Habsburg rule did little, however, to ameliorate the condition of the peasants, who continued to work as serfs for mainly Muslim landlords.

Historical boundaries in the Balkans bore as little relationship to nationality as in the Habsburg Empire. The population of Bosnia-Herzegovina was divided between Orthodox Serbs, Catholic Croats, and Muslims, with no group forming a majority. Between Bosnia-Herzegovina and the Adriatic lay the kingdom of Croatia, which was joined to Hungary and governed from Budapest. A quarter of Croatia's population was made up of Serbs, who mostly lived in the territory of the old military frontier.

Politicians in Croatia increasingly chafed under Hungarian rule from Budapest. Whereas in the past much effort had been wasted in rivalry between Serbs and Croats, in 1903 a so-called 'Croat–Serb Coalition' took power in the Croatian parliament. The Coalition pushed not only for an extension of home rule but also to enlarge Croatia by incorporating Dalmatia, hitherto run from Vienna, and Bosnia-Herzegovina. The 'trialist solution', which envisaged the Empire being divided in three, with its capitals in Vienna, Budapest, and Zagreb in Croatia, was supported by the heir to the throne, Franz Ferdinand (Figure 9). Franz Ferdinand, besides

König Amenhotepp XXIII
Pharao v. Aegypten

9. Franz Ferdinand dressed as an embalmed Egyptian Pharaoh, during his world tour 1892–3. Franz Ferdinand's assassination in 1914 set in train the events that led to the First World War.

being a maniacal huntsman who bagged an estimated 270,000 creatures (mostly partridges, but including two elephants), was convinced that the Habsburg Empire depended for survival on its comprehensive reorganization.

To the east of Bosnia-Herzegovina was the kingdom of Serbia, which had over the course of the 19th century acquired both territory and independence from the Ottoman Empire. Serbia's rulers were increasingly hostile to the Habsburg Empire and they nurtured the ambition ultimately to include all Serbs within the boundaries of the kingdom. Since there was a substantial Serb population in Bosnia-Herzegovina, Croatia, and southern Hungary, Serbian political goals threatened the Habsburg Empire.

Bosnia-Herzegovina thus stood at the centre of rivalries. On the one side, the Croat–Serb Coalition vied to incorporate it in a reshaped Habsburg Empire; on the other, Serbia looked to absorb all or part of the province. Ottoman Turkey had also not forgotten that the province belonged to it. When in 1908 a revolution in Istanbul introduced constitutional reform, the new Turkish government proposed that the population of Bosnia-Herzegovina be allowed to join in the vote for an Ottoman parliament.

The Habsburg military occupation of Bosnia-Herzegovina was intended only as a temporary solution. In what might be considered a masterstroke had it not been performed in such a botched manner, the province was formally annexed in October 1908 and incorporated in the Habsburg Empire. The Habsburg Foreign Minister believed he had the agreement of his Russian counterpart to the annexation, but this was a misunderstanding. The consequence was a breakdown in diplomatic relations, which drew Russia closer to Serbia. Serbian expansion southwards into Ottoman Macedonia during the Balkan Wars of 1912–13 fuelled the suspicion in Vienna that, with Russia's backing,

Serbia would soon seek to 'liberate' the Serbs who lived within the Habsburg Empire.

Serbia had a parliament, elected on a wide franchise, but its government was not democratic. The institutions of state had been eaten away by secret societies and terrorist groups operating from within the army and security services. It was the chief of Serbian military intelligence, Dragutin Dimitrijević, who armed and trained the young terrorists who murdered Franz Ferdinand and his wife on their official visit to Sarajevo in June 1914. Dimitrijević disregarded Serbian government policy, which opposed for the time being all hostile acts against Serbia's more powerful neighbour.

In 1879, the Habsburg Empire had joined Germany in a military alliance aimed against Russia. The alliance languished, seldom amounting to more than an exchange of Christmas cards between the Habsburg and German general staffs. Emperor Wilhelm II, however, now gave Franz Joseph his full backing to take military action against Serbia. Wilhelm had no intention of starting a world war, but there were plenty of generals and others within the political establishment in Vienna who viewed a European conflict with enthusiasm, as presaging 'a totally new epoch' in which the Empire's fortunes would be restored. Even though they knew that attacking Serbia must lead to Russian intervention, they convinced Franz Joseph that he had no alternative but to fight. By August 1914, most of Europe was at war.

The First World War

Posters written in fifteen languages announced the mobilization of the Habsburg armed forces. From the very first, the problem ⸺s not only the logistical one of how to move over a million ⸺alf men to the front but also one of morale—of how to ⸺ different national groups to fight. The officer ⸺ army may well have been enthused by an 'imperial patriotism' that looked beyond nationality, but the rank and file were not so moved. A sense of Habsburg identity and belonging was singularly missing and recent attempts to promote it had fallen flat. On the occasion of Franz Joseph's sixtieth official birthday, in 1908, Czechs, Italians, and Hungarians had boycotted the ceremony, while the 'procession of the nations', intended to pay homage to the emperor, had amounted to little more than a handful of cavorting Carinthians in colourful costumes.

The solution was to appeal to national sentiments. Recruits were accordingly allowed to mass under their own national flags and they were lured by the prospect of going to war against their nation's traditional enemy—Poles against Russians, Croats against Serbs, Hungarians against Slavs of all types, and so on. On the home front, the work of sustaining the injured, bereaved, and orphaned was allocated to national associations, which administered welfare payments and staffed the boards that appointed guardians. Appeals to nationalism seemed to work and some commentators noted with surprise 'the frenetic rejoicing, with music and song' that greeted troops on their way to war. Elsewhere, however, enthusiasm was muted—only fourteen students enlisted from the whole of Prague. In other Bohemian towns, up to three-quarters of Czechs who were mustered suddenly contracted debilitating illnesses.

Motivated more by national hatreds than by a sombre patriotism, Habsburg forces frequently ran amok, slaughtering civilians and burning villages. One typical order, issued in September 1914, on the Russian front, in response to a report that some villagers had ambushed troops read, 'Pull out the mayor, priest, assistant priest and a few others, principally Jews, and shoot them immediately. Then burn the place and try to knock down the church steeple.' As this instruction suggests, even the hostility of the officer corps to antisemitism (17 per cent of Habsburg officers were Jews) was breaking down.

Desperation fed excess. The Habsburg armies were ill equipped and poorly trained—only one in twenty adult males had received any military instruction before 1914, and for most this had been perfunctory. The trains that conveyed the men to the front travelled no faster than bicycles; provisioning was haphazard, and tin lids substituted for spades. The infantry did at least wear camouflage grey, although officers were still tripped up by their compulsory dress swords. Much can be blamed on financial exigency. The generals, however, were incompetent. Halfway through mobilization in August 1914, the Habsburg chief-of-staff, Conrad von Hötzendorf, reversed his plans, which left an entire army stranded on the Serbian as opposed to the Russian front, where it should have been. The campaign against Serbia, launched in August, was conducted according to a battle plan which, when it had been war-gamed, had been shown to fail.

The war on the Russian or Eastern Front was more mobile than on the Western, and Habsburg forces were deployed along a 1,000-kilometre line. To begin with, the Russians made rapid gains, coming almost within a day's march of Cracow and destroying half the army's regular troops—hereafter it would depend on hastily trained conscripts. Then came the Italian declaration of war in May 1915, which forced the deployment of Habsburg troops to the Alps, and in the summer of 1916 a crushing Russian offensive, which convinced Romania to enter the war against the Habsburgs. To withstand the Russians, the Habsburg armies depended on German reinforcements, which had to be rushed from the siege of the French fortress of Verdun to support their ally. The Habsburg Empire became the military appendage of Germany, the strategic command of its forces passing in September 1916 to Emperor Wilhelm II.

Backed by the Germans, the next two years were for the Habsburgs crowned with military successes. The Serbian army, already in retreat, abandoned the Balkan mainland for the Greek Ionian Islands. The Romanians were defeated and forced in December

1917 to sue for peace, while Russia collapsed into revolution. The Italian front held and Venice lay within the Habsburg military grasp. As the Habsburg Foreign Minister reported in November 1917, 'the war can be regarded as won'.

The home front, nevertheless, deteriorated. Starvation, rationing, and food queues gave way to strikes and bread riots. In January 1918, 700,000 workers downed tools for ten days, while tens of thousands more gathered to listen to agitators. In the spring of 1918, Cracow dissolved into mayhem as Jewish shops were plundered and fights for food spilled onto the streets. In order to feed the population, local officials often requisitioned supplies intended for the army. Although there was no nationalist revolt on the scale of the Irish Easter Rising or a mutiny as serious as the French army's in the middle of 1917, there was the constant drip of insubordination, desertion, and draft-dodging. By early 1918, the Hungarian authorities alone were looking for 200,000 deserters. Large swathes of the countryside became ungovernable as those on the run turned to brigandage.

Although numerically depleted, the bulk of the Habsburg armed forces stayed at least disciplined. When in early November 1918 the Italian army took the surrender of around 400,000 Habsburg troops, it discovered that they included more than 80,000 Czechs and Slovaks, 60,000 South Slavs (mostly Croats), 25,000 Transylvanian Romanians, and even 7,000 Italians from Istria and the Tyrol. It was the final irony that as the Empire dissolved into national units, its army retained its multi-national character.

The last emperor

On 21 November 1916, Franz Joseph died. His last reported words were to his valet: 'Tomorrow morning, at half past three.' Although sick, the 86-year-old emperor was determined to rise at his usual time. Franz Joseph's successor was his nephew Karl. The new ruler fell short of the standard set by his uncle. As a contemporary quip put it, 'You hope to meet a thirty-year-old man, but you find the appearance of a twenty-year-old youth, who thinks, speaks, and acts like a ten-year-old boy.'

Notwithstanding these jibes, Karl was a decent man, committed to peace. But he lacked both the authority that age had lent his predecessor and the tenacity of Franz Ferdinand, into whose inheritance he had stepped. Karl's dislike of Jews and socialists robbed him, moreover, of advisers of imagination. Instead, he made do with a fast-moving stream of mediocre bureaucrats and aristocrats, whom he dismissed as soon as they had proved their incompetence. Moreover, he seemed resigned to failure. On a visit to the General Staff headquarters in spring 1915, he was reported to have said that he did 'not understand why we make so much effort, since everything is in any case pointless, for the war cannot be won'.

On previous occasions, when faced with military disaster the Habsburgs had made peace, even at the price of surrendering lands and the occasional princess. To win their support, the Western allies had promised Italy and Romania slices of the Habsburg Empire—Transylvania, and the southern Tyrol and Dalmatia respectively. The Habsburg Empire could have borne these losses. It might even have survived the sacrifice of part of Galicia, had this been the price of peace with Russia. By 1916, however, the Habsburg Empire's fate was bound to Germany's and many of its troops were now under the command of German generals.

Although Emperor Karl put out feelers to test whether a peace might be obtained, his overtures to London and Paris came to nothing. In order to reassure the German emperor, the Habsburg Foreign Minister publicly affirmed in April 1918 that Karl had no interest in making a separate peace. The next month, Karl visited Emperor Wilhelm and agreed not only to the further coordination of their armies under German command but also to the Habsburg Empire's subordination to Germany's economic policy and expansive war aims.

In April 1917, the United States had entered the war. To begin with, President Woodrow Wilson had no intention of breaking up the Habsburg Empire. His 'Fourteen Points', outlined in January 1918, spoke only of giving the peoples of the Empire 'the freest opportunity to autonomous development'. Lloyd George, the British Prime Minister, also declared that the dismantling of the Empire was 'no part of our war aims'. But with little prospect of detaching the Habsburg Empire from Germany, the allied position hardened. The US Secretary of State demanded that the Empire 'be wiped off the map of Europe' and in June 1918 Wilson declared that 'all branches of the Slav race must be completely liberated from German and Austrian domination'. Allied propaganda now openly supported the Empire's dissolution and its replacement by independent nation states.

In May 1917, Karl had reconvened the parliament in Vienna and two months later he had declared a general amnesty, releasing over 2,000 political prisoners. Many of these favoured the Empire's comprehensive refashioning and even its obliteration. Ideas that had previously been marginal were now amplified on the floor of the Reichsrat. The first was that all South Slavs should be united in a single state that brought together Slovenes, Croats, and Serbs, and which would be powerful enough to head off Italian claims to the Adriatic seaboard. Championed by a South Slav Committee, which operated in exile, the dream of a united 'Yugoslav' state was endorsed by the Serbian government. The second was the vision of Tomáš Masaryk, the future president of Czechoslovakia, that Czechs and Slovaks should join together in a single state. Exiled in London, Masaryk gradually convinced British politicians that his scheme was not fanciful.

Western leaders recognized that after the war they might need a strong Austrian state as a counterweight to Germany. For the time being, however, they were ready to sacrifice the Habsburg Empire in order to speed up an end to hostilities. In the summer of 1918, France, Britain, and the United States recognized the South Slav Committee and the exiled Czechoslovak Committee, led by Masaryk, as the provisional governments in their respective parts of the Habsburg Empire.

The end came swiftly, with the failure of the German summer offensive on the Western Front. Early on in October 1918, the German government began negotiations for a ceasefire. Their fates militarily intertwined, Germany's defeat became the Habsburg Empire's too. In a vain attempt to accommodate demands for self-government, Emperor Karl issued a manifesto that attempted to restructure the Empire on national lines. But representatives of the national committees seized power in Prague and elsewhere, claiming that they should be regarded as the governments constituted by the manifesto. At the end of the month, a revolution in Hungary brought into power the socialist leader, the 'Red Count' Michael Károlyi.

Not much was left of the Habsburg Empire. Even in the Austrian lands, an independent 'German-Austrian State' was proclaimed, which declared a republic. On 11 November, Emperor Karl formally relinquished his involvement in public affairs (he did not abdicate). Shortly afterwards, the Austrian socialist leader, Karl Renner, visited Emperor Karl in the Schönbrunn palace, bidding him speed with the words, 'Herr Habsburg, the taxi is waiting'—probably the first time in 500 years that a Habsburg ruler had been so addressed.

Karl twice sought in 1921 to seize power in Hungary as its rightful king, but he was repulsed. He died the next year, in exile in Madeira, where he was laid to rest. In accordance with Habsburg tradition, Karl's heart was buried separately. Since it could not be interred in a church in Vienna, it was brought to the Swiss abbey of Muri, close to the old Habsburg Castle. After eight centuries, the dynasty had returned in death to the countryside of its birth.

Rethinking the Habsburg Empire

History is written by the victors. The victor in the 19th century was the modern centralized state. The victor in the next was the national state. The Habsburg Empire was neither centralized nor national. It remained in the form it had acquired in the 16th century—a collection of disparate lands, kingdoms, and peoples united by a common monarch and ruling house. Not surprisingly, 'ramshackle' is the cliché which historians most often use to describe the Empire, along with 'anachronistic'. Some may quote with approval the satirist Karl Kraus's incomprehensible but lofty verdict that the Habsburg Empire was 'the research laboratory for world destruction'; others repeat a German Foreign Minister's assessment, delivered in 1914, that it was 'an ever increasingly disintegrating composition of nations'.

Even at the time, there were plenty of politicians and commentators who had plans for the Empire's reorganization. Most of their schemes were based on decentralization and on some sort of federal arrangement, by which nationality would be squared with territory. One plan, proposed in 1906 by the Transylvanian Romanian Aurel Popovici, was for a 'United States of Greater Austria', which envisaged the Empire being divided into fifteen provinces, each with a dominant national majority. Another posited a 'personal principle', by which people would be organized in loose national associations, which would oversee educational and cultural policy, while territorial units looked after less contentious administrative matters. Promoted by the socialist leaders Karl Renner and Otto Bauer, the so-called 'Austro-Marxist solution' provided much of the thinking behind Belgium's present constitutional organization.

As the recommendations of Popovici, Renner, and Bauer suggest, the centralized state was not the only political choice available at the start of the 20th century. The example of the federal United

States and Switzerland had until a few decades before been a bad one. But once recovered from their respective civil wars (albeit a brief one in Switzerland's case), and with now burgeoning economies, the two countries were in their political arrangements seen to offer a solution to states with complex populations. There was nothing untimely, therefore, about the Habsburg Empire's decentralized and non-unitary character. In the context of the early 20th century, it represented one way forward, which could (or so it was thought) be adjusted and improved upon.

Nor was the Habsburg Empire unusual in being multinational. Most states in the 19th century were. Germany had three million Poles within its borders, concentrated in the east, while less than a half of the population of Tsarist Russia counted as Russians (by a convenient sleight, Ukrainians were defined as 'Little Russians'). Indeed, most of the states which took the place of the Habsburg Empire were similarly multinational. One-third of the populations of inter-war Poland and Romania was neither Polish nor Romanian, and two-fifths of Czechoslovakia was neither Czech nor Slovak. In its earliest incarnation as the Kingdom of the Serbs, Croats, and Slovenes, Yugoslavia was expressly multinational.

The differences were twofold. First, most European states, both before and after the First World War, acted as if they were made up of one nation and they used the educational system, army, and bureaucracy to impose a single identity. The Hungarian government attempted this after 1867, without success. Elsewhere in the Habsburg Empire acculturation through the school system was embarked upon only in a few localities where one national group formed a majority (and even then subject to review by the Constitutional Court). But the task was simply too great and, in any case, to what group were the target nations to be assimilated in a population where no one group had a majority? (German-speakers made up less than a quarter of the overall population; Hungarian-speakers about a fifth.)

The first point leads to the second. No other European state, with the exception of the Ottoman Empire and Tsarist Russia, had so many national groups and in such abundance. Moreover, some of these had kinsmen just across the border, who sustained their sense of separate belonging and nurtured irredentist sentiments. As the Hungarian leader, Louis Kossuth, recognized in exile, the only way of resolving the problem of diversity and kinship in Hungary and the northern Balkans was a Great Danube Confederation, which would loosely unite the 30 million inhabitants of Hungary, Romania, and Serbia 'in a first-class state, rich and powerful and one that will weigh heavily in Europe's balance'. Even so, he offered no solution for the lands and kingdoms on this side of the Leitha.

The Habsburg Empire was not an anachronism. It represented in its multinational composition only an extreme example of a condition that was endemic across Europe in the 19th and early 20th centuries. Heterogeneity of population would only be resolved in Central Europe in the middle decades of the 20th century by border changes and the movement of cattle trucks with human cargo.

The same consideration of 'extreme in its ordinariness' applies to other aspects of the Habsburg Empire and the collective history of the Habsburg lands. The Habsburg territories were acquired through marriage and war, which was usual enough in the Middle Ages and early modern period. But no dynasty was as tenacious and fortunate in its acquisitions as the Habsburgs, nor so determined to create a mystique and mythology around its history. The Habsburg possessions constituted, like most other dynastic assemblages, a 'composite monarchy', made up of many parts, but the dynasty outperformed all others in the complexity and geographic spread of its territories. Its rulers embraced the politics of confession in the 17th century, but did so even to the extent of taking Europe into three decades of war. In the next century, the Habsburgs produced Joseph II, who was 'perhaps the completest enlightened despot in European history'.

The Habsburg Empire collapsed as a consequence of the First World War. It was not alone in its dissolution. The Ottoman Empire and Tsarist Russia also fell apart, as did British rule in the 'home territory' of Ireland. In the Habsburg Empire's demise too, there was ordinariness, but one which is barbed by our knowledge of what is to follow—authoritarian rule, fascism, mass murder, communism, and post-communist kleptocracy.

Franz Joseph had to put up with much from Hungarians. On one occasion, the Hungarian Count Kállay drew the emperor's attention to the antiquity of the Kállay family, which, as he proudly explained, had produced great lords at a time when Franz Joseph's forebears were just minor barons in Switzerland. 'Yes, but we have done rather better,' the emperor replied. Where the Habsburg Empire once stood in Central Europe are now thirteen republics. Many of these are ruled by thugs and thieves, who have plundered their populations. The Habsburgs, indeed, did rather better.

References

Chapter 1: Dynasties and empires; titles and peoples

On the spelling of Franz Joseph's name, see the diplomas in the foyer of the Wiener Musikverein concert hall in Vienna, signed by the emperor in both styles.

On Emperor Sigismund's insult to Ernest, see Jakob Unrest, *Österreichische Chronik*, ch. 5, in MGH, Scrip. rer. Germ., ns, xi, 4.

On the history of the Holy Roman Empire, see now Joachim Whaley, *Germany and the Holy Roman Empire*, 2 vols (Oxford, 2013), and Peter H. Wilson, *The Holy Roman Empire: A Thousand Years of Europe's History* (London, 2016).

'While others fight...' The origins of this adage are uncertain. It is probably of early 16th-century origin. It ultimately derives from Ovid's *Heroides*.

On the titles used in 1648, see F. G. Davenport, *European Treaties bearing on the History of the United States* (Washington, DC, 1917), 361; *Quellen zur Geschichte des Völkerrechts*, ed. W. G. Grewe, vol. 2 (Berlin and New York, 1988), 183–4.

On the idea of dynasty, see Jeroen Duindam, *Dynasties: A Global History of Power, 1300–1800* (Cambridge, 2015), and *Dynastic Identity in Early Modern Europe*, ed. Liesbeth Geevers and Mirella Marini (Farnham and Burlington, Vt, 2015), especially the editors' introduction, 1–23.

Charles II of Spain had only sixteen out of a possible twenty-four great-grandparents and great-great-grandparents. Historians who give him fewer have confused two different women called Maria Anna of Bavaria.

On audiences, see Philip Mansel, *Prince of Europe: The Life of Charles-Joseph de Ligne* (London, 2003), 157.

The comment by Leopold II is taken from Wandruszka, *House of Habsburg* (London, 1964), 148.

Chapter 2: The imperial vision: 11th to 16th century

The Latin text of Julius's charter is given in Gerhart Ladner, 'The Middle Ages in Austrian Tradition', *Viator*, 3 (1972), 443–4.

On early landholding on the Upper Rhine, see Tom Scott, *Regional Identity and Economic Change: The Upper Rhine 1450–1600* (Oxford, 1997), 17–50.

On Rudolf IV and St Leopold, see Ronald C. Finucane, *Contested Canonizations: The Last Medieval Saints, 1482–1523* (Washington, DC, 2011), 73–4.

On Frederick III, see Heinrich Koller, *Kaiser Friedrich III* (Darmstadt, 2005); also F. R. H. Du Boulay, *Germany in the Later Middle Ages* (London, 1983), 54–63.

The *Chronicle of the 95 Lords* is given in MGH SS, Dt. Chron., 6.

The classic exposition of AEIOU is by Alphons Lhotsky, in his *Aufsätze und Vorträge*, vol. 2 (Vienna, 1971), 164–222, but see also Heinrich Koller, 'Zur Bedeutung des Vokalspiels AEIOU', *Österreich in Geschichte und Literatur*, 39, no. 3 (1995), 162–70.

On Maximilian I, see Gerhard Benecke, *Maximilian I (1459–1519): An Analytical Biography* (London, 1982), which includes his itinerary; also, Larry Silver, *Marketing Maximilian: The Visual Ideology of a Holy Roman Emperor* (Princeton and Oxford, 2008).

'It is very pusillanimous…' See James D. Tracey, *Emperor Charles V, Impresario of War: Campaign Strategy, International Finance, and Domestic Politics* (Cambridge, 2002), 21.

'I have been nine times to Germany…' See Henry Kamen, *Philip of Spain* (New Haven and London, 1997), 63. Charles had visited England in 1520 and 1522 in order to secure Henry VIII's support ⟨agai⟩nst France.

⟨Chapt⟩er 3: 'As if the king of each': 16th and 17th centuries

⟨On th⟩e idea of the 'last emperor', see Anke Holdenried, *The Sibyl ⟨an⟩d her Scribes: Manuscripts and Interpretation of the Latin ⟨Si⟩bylla Tiburtina c.1050–1500* (Aldershot and Burlington, ⟨Vermon⟩t, 2006).

'We who are as good as you are': see Henry Kamen, *Spain 1469-1714: A Society of Conflict* (Harlow, 1983), 14.

On the coronation in Bohemia, see Benita Berning, *'Nach alltem löblichen Gebrauch'. Die böhmischen Königskrönungen der Frühen Neuzeit (1526-1743)* (Cologne, 2008).

'Presumption is always': see James D. Tracy, *Holland under Habsburg Rule, 1506-1566* (Berkeley, 1990), 50.

On the court ordinance of 1527 and its limits, see Eduard Rosenthal, *Die Behördeorganisation Kaiser Ferdinands I.* (Vienna, 1887).

'But a ceremony': reported by Edward Herbert (1583-1648), in *Life of Lord Herbert, of Cherbury* (London, 1856), 252.

On the Spanish Riding School and Lipizzaner horses, see Mathilde Windisch-Graetz, *The Spanish Riding School* (London, 1956).

For the Escorial Palace, see Henry Kamen, *The Escorial: Art and Power in the Renaissance* (New Haven, 2010).

'Rather than suffer the least injury': see Henry Kamen, *Philip of Spain* (New Haven and London, 1997), 115.

'Every individual has the feeling': see Kamen, *Philip of Spain*, 123.

On Jewish Prague, see Hillel J. Kieval, *Languages of Community: The Jewish Experience in the Czech Lands* (Berkeley, Los Angeles, and London, 2000).

On the Reformation in Habsburg Central Europe, see contributions in *A Companion to the Reformation in Central Europe*, ed. Howard Louthan and Graeme Murdock (Leiden, 2015).

'His Majesty is interested': see R. J. W. Evans, *Rudolf II and his World: A Study in Intellectual History, 1576-1612* (Oxford, 1973), 167.

On Transylvania, see Graeme Murdock, *Calvinism and the Reformed Church in Hungary and Transylvania c.1600-1660* (Oxford, 2000).

On the costs of warfare in Hungary, see *Magyar történet 1526-1686*, ed. Zsigmond Pál Pach, vol. 1 (Budapest, 1985), 429; István Kenyeres, *Uradalmak és végvárak* (Budapest, 2008).

On military technology and the Habsburg–Ottoman wars, see Gábor Ágoston, 'Habsburgs and Ottomans: Defense, Military Change and Shifts in Power', *Turkish Studies Association Bulletin*, 22, no. 1 (1998), 126–41.

Chapter 4: In the service of the faith: 17th and 18th centuries

'Nothing sown': see Geoffrey Parker, *The Thirty Years' War* (London, 1984), 39.

'A triumph of management': see Bernd Rill, *Kaiser Matthias. Bruderzwist und Glaubenskampf* (Graz, Vienna, and Cologne, 1999), 287.

'An irregular body': coined by Samuel Pufendorf (1632–94) and frequently misunderstood. See Hanns Gross, *Empire and Sovereignty: A History of the Public Law Literature in the Holy Roman Empire, 1599–1804* (Chicago and London, 1973), 321–6.

On 'squeezing the Hungarians into Bohemian breeches', see Martyn Rady, *Customary Law in Hungary: Courts, Texts and the Tripartitum* (Oxford, 2015), 176.

On Fóris Otrokócsi, see Graeme Murdock, 'Responses to Habsburg Persecution of Protestants in Seventeenth-Century Hungary', *Austrian History Yearbook*, 40 (2009), 37–52.

'So that the kingdom or at least a good part of it': see *Einrichtungswerk des Königreichs Hungarn (1688–1690)*, ed. János Kálmár and János J. Varga (Stuttgart, 2010), 74.

For the history of the Banat, see Irina Marin, *Contested Frontiers in the Balkans: Habsburg and Ottoman Rivalries in Eastern Europe* (London, 2013).

On Martin Cortés, son of the conqueror of Mexico, Hernán Cortés, see Hugh Thomas, *World Without End: The Global Empire of Philip II* (London, 2014), 76.

On slavery in the Spanish New World, see *Encyclopedia Africana*, 2nd edn, vol. 4 (Oxford, 2005), 786–8.

On the European baroque, see now Peter Hersche, *Musse und Verschwendung. Europäische Gesellschaft und Kultur im Barockzeitalter*, 2 vols (Freiburg, Basel, and Vienna, 2006), and Hersche, *Gelassenheit und Lebensfreude. Was wir vom Barock lernen können* (Freiburg, Basel, and Vienna, 2011).

For 'Austrian piety' and its staging, see Anna Coreth, *Pietas Austriaca*, trans. D. Bowman and Anna Maria Leitgeb (West Lafayette, Ind., 2004).

On 'refeudalization' in Spain, see *The Castilian Crisis of the Seventeenth Century*, ed. I. A. A. Thompson and Bartolomé Yun Casalilla (Cambridge, 1994), 249–76.

On debt peonage, see Hermann W. Konrad, *A Jesuit Hacienda in Colonial Mexico: Santa Lucia, 1576–1767* (Stanford, Calif., 1980), 282.

Chapter 5: Enlightenment and reaction: 18th and 19th centuries

'We are forever only giving foreigners': cited by Graeme Murdock in *Under Eastern Eyes: A Comparative Introduction to East European Travel Writing in Europe*, ed. Wendy Bracewell and Alex Drace-Francis (Budapest and New York, 2008), 125. For Hörnigk's *Austria Over All*, see *The Habsburg and Hohenzollern Dynasties in the Seventeenth and Eighteenth Centuries*, ed. C. A. Macartney (New York, Evanston, Ill., and London, 1970), 70–8.

For cameralism, see Keith Tribe, 'Cameralism and the Science of Government', *Journal of Modern History*, 56, no. 2 (1984), 263–84; Andre Wakefield, 'Cameralism: A German Alternative to Mercantilism', in *Mercantilism Reimagined*, ed. Philip J. Stern and Carl Wennerlind (Oxford, 2014), 134–50.

On natural law, see T. J. Hochstrasser, *Natural Law Theories in the Early Enlightenment* (Cambridge, 2000).

'Every tradition which has no justifiable basis': Joseph von Sonnenfels, given in T. C. W. Blanning, *Joseph II and Enlightened Despotism* (London, 1970), 3.

'All the duties of peoples': Von Justi, given in Peter Gay, *The Enlightenment: The Science of Freedom* (New York and London, 1968), 489.

For the contemporary understanding of despotism, see Derek Beales, *Joseph II*, vol. 2 (Cambridge, 2013), 656.

On Gypsies, see Becky Taylor, *Another Darkness, Another Dawn: A History of Gypsies, Roma and Travellers* (London, 2014). The absence of records and problems of identity and definition make it impossible to state the size of the Gypsy population with any certainty. In the Habsburg Empire it was in 1900 put at 300,000, which is almost certainly an underestimate.

On Galicia, see Horst Glassl, *Die österreichische Einrichtungswerk in Galizien (1772–1790)* (Wiesbaden, 1975).

On the loose women of Vienna, see *The Life of David Hume*, ed. E. C. Mossner, 2nd edn (Oxford, 1980), 211.

For 'silliness and ignorance', see Gábor Klaniczay, 'Decline of Witches and Rise of Vampires in 18th Century Habsburg Monarchy', *Ethnologia Europaea*, 17 (1987), 165–80.

References

On Joseph II's biblioclasm, see Friedrich Buchmayr, in *Lost Libraries: The Destruction of Great Book Collections since Antiquity*, ed. James Raven (Basingstoke and New York, 2004).

On censorship, see Leslie Bodi, *Tauwetter in Wien. Zur Prosa der österreichischen Aufklärung 1781–1795* (Vienna, Cologne, and Weimar, 1995), 51.

On 'more and more conversations', see James Van Horn Melton, *The Rise of the Public in Enlightenment Europe* (Cambridge, 2001), 243.

On the Viennese masonic lodges, see *Die Protokolle der Wiener Freimaurerloge 'Zum wahren Eintracht' (1781–1785)*, ed. Hans-Josef Irmen (Frankfurt am Main, 1994). For freemasonry in Bohemia, I am indebted to Helena Braeuerová, *The Origin and Early Development of Freemasonry in Bohemia from the Earliest Times to 1795*, unpublished MA dissertation, University of London, 1992.

'The people aren't just bog roll' is taken from Franz Hebenstreit's *Eipeldauer Song* (1793). For the specially trained dogs, see Tim Blanning, *The Pursuit of Glory, Europe 1648–1815* (London, 2007), 299.

'Your repressive and suffocating policy': see Alan Sked, *The Decline and Fall of the Habsburg Empire* (London and New York, 1989), 10.

Chapter 6: The era of Franz Joseph: 19th century

For the students' flag, see Theodor Gomperz, *Essays und Erinnerungen* (Stuttgart and Leipzig, 1905), 19.

On the history of the Pan-Slav Congress, see Lawrence D. Orton, *The Prague Slav Congress of 1848* (Boulder, Colo., and New York, 1978).

For Latour's controversial role, see Josef Polišenský, *Aristocrats and the Crowd in the Revolutionary Year 1848* (Albany, NY, 1980), 139.

On Radetzky's (mostly unsuccessful) deployment of 200 hot-air balloons against Venice, see R. T. C. Rolt, *The Aeronauts: A History of Ballooning 1783–1903* (Gloucester, 1985), 165.

Karl von Frankenstein's death was reported in the *Grazer Zeitung*, 7 July 1848. It is not chronologically possible that he inspired Mary Shelley's *Frankenstein*, published in 1818.

One of Franz Joseph's mistresses kept a diary. See *Anna Nahowski und Kaiser Franz Josef*, ed. Herwig Knaus (Vienna, 2012).

The literature on nationalism in the Habsburg Empire is extensive. Recent works are conveniently distilled in Jonathan Kwan,

'Nationalism and all that: Reassessing the Habsburg Monarchy and its Legacy', *European History Quarterly*, 41, no. 1 (2011), 88–92. On 'everyday' nationalism, see Alexander Maxwell, '"The Handsome Man with Hungarian Moustache and Beard": National Moustaches in Habsburg Hungary', *Journal of Cultural and Social History*, vol. 12, no. 1 (2015), 51–76; Maxwell, 'National Alcohol in Hungary's Reform Era: Wine, Spirits, and the Patriotic Imagination', *Central Europe*, vol. 12, no. 2 (2014), 117–35.

'Keeping the nationalities': Von Taaffe, given in C. A. Macartney, *History of the Habsburg Empire 1790–1918*, 2nd edn (London, 1971), 615.

For the comments by Berta Szeps-Zuckerkandl and the Culture Minister, Wilhelm von Hartel, see Carl E. Schorske, *Fin-de-siècle Vienna: Politics and Culture* (Cambridge, 1981), 237.

For Csokor's *3 November 1918*, see Jamie A. M. Bulloch, *The Promotion of an Austrian Identity 1918–1938*, online PhD thesis (University College London, 2002), 207.

Chapter 7: World war and dissolution: 20th century

Franz Ferdinand has been badly served by historians. But see Gordon Brook-Shepherd, *Victims at Sarajevo: The Romance and Tragedy of Franz Ferdinand and Sophie* (London, 1984). Franz Ferdinand's travel diaries indicate a sensitive and shrewd observer. See *Tagebuch meiner Reise um die Erde 1892–1893*, ed. Franz Gerbert (Vienna, 2013).

Historians all tell us of the supra-national ethos of the Habsburg officer corps: thus, István Deák, *Beyond Nationalism: A Social and Political History of the Habsburg Officer Corps 1848–1918* (New York and Oxford, 1992). But see Oberst Bauer, *Der grosse Krieg in Feld und Heimat. Erinnerungen und Betrachtungen*, 3rd edn (Tübingen, 1922), 80.

On processions and festivals, see Nancy Wingfield, *Flag Wars and Stone Saints: How the Bohemian Lands Became Czech* (Cambridge, Mass., and London, 2007).

'Pull out the mayor': Alexander Watson, *Ring of Steel: Germany and Austria-Hungary at War, 1914–1918* (London, 2014), 153.

On Foreign Minister Czernin's optimism, see F. R. Bridge, *The Habsburg Monarchy among the Great Powers, 1815–1918* (New York, Oxford, and Munich, 1990), 364.

Figures on the composition of the army captured in 1918 are given in Alan Sked, *The Decline and Fall of the Habsburg Empire 1815–1918* (London and New York, 1989), 261.

On Emperor Karl's pessimism, see Manfried Rauchensteiner, *The First World War and the End of the Habsburg Monarchy*, 2nd edn (Vienna, Cologne, and Weimar, 2014), 643. On Karl, see now Christopher Brennan, *Reforming Austria-Hungary: Beyond his Control or Beyond his Capacity? The Domestic Politics of Emperor Karl I, November 1916–May 1917*, online PhD thesis (London School of Economics, 2012).

On the growing hostility of the allies, see Bridge, *The Habsburg Monarchy among the Great Powers*, 368. For the propaganda war, see Mark Cornwall, *The Undermining of Austria-Hungary: The Battle for Hearts and Minds* (Basingstoke, 2000).

'Increasingly disintegrating composition': Imanuel Geiss, *July 1914: The Outbreak of the First World War. Selected Documents* (London, 1967), 122.

On Kossuth's Danubian Confederation, see *History of Transylvania*, ed. Béla Köpeczi, vol. 3 (New York, 2002), 426; Ian D. Armour, 'Kossuth's Pie in the Sky: Serbia and the Great Danubian Confederation Scam', in *Lajos Kossuth Sent Word...Papers Delivered on the Occasion of the Bicentenary of Kossuth's Birth*, ed. László Péter, Martyn Rady, and Peter Sherwood (London, 2003), 183–204.

'Completest enlightened despot': see C. A. Macartney, *History of the Habsburg Empire 1790–1918*, 2nd edn (London, 1971), 119.

Kállay's conversation with Franz Joseph was related to me by the late László Péter.

Further reading

General works

F. R. Bridge, *The Habsburg Monarchy among the Great Powers, 1815–1918* (New York, Oxford, and Munich, 1990).

R. J. W. Evans, *The Making of the Habsburg Monarchy, 1550–1700: An Interpretation* (Oxford, 1979).

R. J. W. Evans, *Austria, Hungary, and the Habsburgs: Central Europe c.1683–1867* (Oxford, 2006).

Paula Sutter Fichtner, *The Habsburgs: Dynasty, Culture and Politics* (London, 2014).

Pieter M. Judson, *The Habsburgs: A New History* (Cambridge, Mass., and London, 2016).

C. A. Macartney, *The Habsburg Empire 1790–1918*, 2nd edn (London, 1971).

Robin Okey, *The Habsburg Monarchy c.1765–1918: From Enlightenment to Eclipse* (Basingstoke and London, 2001).

Alan Sked, *The Decline and Fall of the Habsburg Empire, 1815–1918* (London and New York, 1989).

A. J. P. Taylor, *The Habsburg Monarchy, 1809–1918* (London, 1948, and many subsequent editions).

Adam Wandruszka, *The House of Austria: Six Hundred Years of a European Dynasty* (London, 1964).

Geoffrey Wheatcroft, *The Habsburgs: Embodying Empire* (London, 1996).

Chapter 2: The imperial vision: 11th to 16th century

Gerhard Benecke, *Maximilian I, 1459–1519: An Analytical Biography* (London, 1982).

Karl Brandi, *The Emperor Charles V: The Growth and Destiny of a Man and of a World-Empire* (London, 1960).

Paula Sutter Fichtner, *Ferdinand I: The Politics of Dynasticism in the Age of the Reformation* (Boulder, Colo., and New York, 1982).

Martyn Rady, *The Emperor Charles V* (London, 1988).

Marie Tanner, *The Last Descendants of Aeneas: The Hapsburgs and the Mythic Image of the Emperor* (New Haven, 1992).

Chapter 3: 'As if the king of each': 16th and 17th centuries

John Adamson (ed.), *The Princely Courts of Europe 1500–1750* (London, 1999).

R. J. W. Evans, *Rudolf II and his World: A Study in Intellectual History* (Oxford, 1973).

Paula Sutter Fichtner, *Emperor Maximilian II* (New Haven and London, 2001).

Henry Kamen, *Philip of Spain* (New Haven and London, 1997).

Gunther E. Rothenberg, *The Austrian Military Frontier in Croatia, 1522–1747* (Urbana, Ill., 1960).

Chapter 4: In the service of the faith: 17th and 18th centuries

Robert Bireley, *Ferdinand II: Counter-Reformation Emperor, 1578–1637* (New York, 2014).

John P. Spielman, *Leopold I of Austria* (London, 1977).

John Stoye, *The Siege of Vienna* (London, 1964).

Hugh Thomas, *World Without End: The Global Empire of Philip II* (London, 2014).

Peter H. Wilson, *Europe's Tragedy: A History of the Thirty Years War* (London, 2009).

Chapter 5: Enlightenment and reaction: 18th and 19th centuries

Éva H. Balázs, *Hungary and the Habsburgs, 1765–1800: An Experiment in Enlightened Absolutism* (Budapest, 1997).

Derek Beales, *Joseph II*, 2 vols (Cambridge, 1987–2009).

T. C. W. Blanning, *Joseph II* (London, 1994).

Alan Sked, *Metternich and Austria: An Evaluation* (Basingstoke, 2008).

The Habsburg Empire

Ernst Wangermann, *From Joseph II to the Jacobin Trials: Government Policy and Public Opinion in the Habsburg Dominions in the Period of the French Revolution*, 2nd edn (London, 1969).

Chapter 6: The era of Franz Joseph: 19th century

Jean-Paul Bled, *Francis Joseph* (Oxford, 1992).

Steven Beller, *Francis Joseph* (London and New York, 1996).

Stephen Beller, *Vienna and the Jews, 1867–1938: A Cultural History* (Cambridge, 1989).

Brigitte Hamann, *Hitler's Vienna: A Dictator's Apprenticeship* (Oxford, 1999).

Rebecca Houze, *Textiles, Fashion and Design Reform in Austria-Hungary before the First World War: Principles of Dress* (Farnham and Burlington, Vt, 2015).

John Lukacs, *Budapest 1900: A Historical Portrait of a City and its Culture* (London, 1989).

Carl E. Schorske, *Fin-de-siècle Vienna: Politics and Culture* (London, 1980).

Chapter 7: World war and dissolution: 20th century

Gordon Brook-Shepherd, *The Last Habsburg* (London 1968).

Mark Cornwall (ed.), *The Last Years of Austria-Hungary: A Multi-National Experiment in Early Twentieth-Century Europe* (Exeter, 2002).

Robin Okey, *Taming Balkan Nationalism: The Habsburg Civilizing Mission in Bosnia, 1878–1914* (Oxford 2007).

Norman Stone, *The Eastern Front* (London, 1975).

Alexander Watson, *Ring of Steel: Germany and Austria-Hungary at War, 1914–1918* (London, 2014).

Index

Index

V

vampires 66
Vasvár, Treaty of (1664) 53
Venice 24, 72, 78, 83, 101
Verdun 100
viceroys 15, 27, 35, 38, 56
Vienna 14–15, 20, 22–3, 30, 36–7,
    41–2, 54, 58, 60, 65, 67–71,
    75–80, 84, 90–3, 95, 97–8,
    103–4 *see also* Spanish Riding
    School
  Congress of 71–2
  Treaty of (1606) 42, 47
  University of 20, 23
Vorarlberg 7, 20

W

Waterloo, battle (1815) 71
Westphalia, Peace of (1648) 51–2
Wiener Neustadt 21–2
Wilhelm II, German emperor 86,
    98, 100, 102

Wilson, Woodrow, US
    President 103
Windischgrätz, Field Marshal 78–81
Winds, nationality 86
witches 66
Wittgenstein, Ludwig,
    philosopher 90
wizards 38, 41, 48
women 14, 35, 38, 87
Work of Instauration 55
World War One *see* First
    World War
Worms, diet of 29

Y

Yiddish 87, 91
Yugoslavia 56, 103, 106
Yuste, monastery 31

Z

Zagreb 77, 95
zoos 37, 92–3

ISLAMIC HISTORY
A Very Short Introduction
Adam J. Silverstein

Does history matter? This book argues not that history matters,
but that Islamic history does. This *Very Short Introduction*
introduces the story of Islamic history; the controversies
surrounding its study; and the significance that it holds - for
Muslims and for non-Muslims alike. Opening with a lucid
overview of the rise and spread of Islam, from the seventh to
twenty first century, the book charts the evolution of what was
originally a small, localised community of believers into an
international religion with over a billion adherents. Chapters
are also dedicated to the peoples - Arabs, Persians, and
Turks - who shaped Islamic history, and to three representative
institutions - the mosque, jihad, and the caliphate - that highlight
Islam's diversity over time.

> 'The book is extremely lucid, readable, sensibly organised, and
> wears its considerable learning, as they say, 'lightly'.'
>
> BBC History Magazine

www.oup.com/vsi

AFRICAN HISTORY
A Very Short Introduction
John Parker & Richard Rathbone

Essential reading for anyone interested in the African continent and the diversity of human history, this *Very Short Introduction* looks at Africa's past and reflects on the changing ways it has been imagined and represented. Key themes in current thinking about Africa's history are illustrated with a range of fascinating historical examples, drawn from over 5 millennia across this vast continent.

'A very well informed and sharply stated historiography...should be in every historiography student's kitbag. A tour de force...it made me think a great deal.'

Terence Ranger,
The Bulletin of the School of Oriental and African Studies

www.oup.com/vsi

GERMAN LITERATURE
A Very Short Introduction
Nicholas Boyle

German writers, from Luther and Goethe to Heine, Brecht, and Günter Grass, have had a profound influence on the modern world. This *Very Short Introduction* presents an engrossing tour of the course of German literature from the late Middle Ages to the present, focussing especially on the last 250 years. Emphasizing the economic and religious context of many masterpieces of German literature, it highlights how they can be interpreted as responses to social and political changes within an often violent and tragic history. The result is a new and clear perspective which illuminates the power of German literature and the German intellectual tradition, and its impact on the wider cultural world.

> 'Boyle has a sure touch and an obvious authority...this is a balanced and lively introduction to German literature.'
>
> **Ben Hutchinson, TLS**

SOCIAL MEDIA
Very Short Introduction

Join our community
www.oup.com/vsi

- Join us online at the official Very Short Introductions **Facebook** page.
- Access the thoughts and musings of our authors with our online **blog**.
- Sign up for our monthly **e-newsletter** to receive information on all new titles publishing that month.
- Browse the full range of Very Short Introductions online.
- Read **extracts** from the Introductions for free.
- Visit our library of **Reading Guides**. These guides, written by our expert authors will help you to question again, why you think what you think.
- If you are a teacher or lecturer you can order inspection copies quickly and simply via our website.

ONLINE CATALOGUE
A Very Short Introduction

Our online catalogue is designed to make it easy to find your ideal Very Short Introduction. View the entire collection by subject area, watch author videos, read sample chapters, and download reading guides.

http://fds.oup.com/www.oup.co.uk/general/vsi/index.html